CULTURE EATS CREATIVITY FOR LUNCH
THE ULKAWAY

Arvind Wable is an alumnus of Mayo College, St. Stephens, Delhi School of Economics and IIM Ahmedabad. His career of almost four decades spanned advertising and marketing in large multinational advertising agencies and start-ups. He served as CEO at FCB Ulka and FCB Singapore.

Arvind has a keen interest in coaching and mentoring. He is a life coach and certified master practitioner in solution-focused coaching.

Arvind is actively involved in social, environmental and conservation issues and is the president of the board of trustees of WWF-India. He also serves on the steering committee of India Sanitation Coalition and advisory boards of SDMH Hospital and Kala Sakshi Memorial Trust. He is an enthusiastic painter and a wildlife photographer.

CULTURE EATS CREATIVITY FOR LUNCH
THE ULKAWAY

Arvind Wable

Published by
Rupa Publications India Pvt. Ltd 2024
7/16, Ansari Road, Daryaganj
New Delhi 110002

Sales Centres:
Bengaluru Chennai Hyderabad
Jaipur Kathmandu Kolkata
Mumbai Prayagraj

Copyright © Arvind Wable 2024
Foreword and diagrams copyright © Kim Cameron 2024
Photographs courtesy: Arvind Wable

Copyright of the photograph vests with the photographer/copyright owner. Copyright of the reproduced advertisements vest with the respective owners of the brands. While every effort has been made to trace copyright holders and obtain permission, this has not been possible in all cases; any omissions brought to our attention will be remedied in future editions.

The views and opinions expressed in this book are the author's own and the facts are as reported by him, which have been verified to the extent possible, and the publishers are not in any way liable for the same.

All rights reserved.

No part of this publication may be reproduced, transmitted or stored in a retrieval system, in any form or by any means, electronic, mechanical, photocopying, recording or otherwise, without the prior permission of the publisher.

P-ISBN: 978-93-6156-794-0
E-ISBN: 978-93-6156-438-3

First impression 2024

10 9 8 7 6 5 4 3 2 1

The moral right of the author has been asserted.

Printed in India

This book is sold subject to the condition that it shall not,
by way of trade or otherwise, be lent, resold, hired out
or otherwise circulated, without the publisher's prior consent,
in any form of binding or cover other than that in which it is published.

To
Anil Kapoor
Billy, Boss, Bhai

CONTENTS

Foreword / ix

Introduction / 1

One: The Beginning / 8

Two: Rise, Fall, Resurrection / 12

Three: Becoming FCB Ulka / 17

Four: Built to Last / 25

Five: Attitude vs Aptitude / 37

Six: Advertising Is a Senior Person's Business / 48

Seven: Never Buy People / 54

Eight: Prima Donnas / 62

Nine: No Zero No Hero Overnight / 68

Ten: No Turf Wars / 76

Eleven: The Ulkaway / 81

Twelve: Strategy vs Creativity / 97

Thirteen: Creating Brand Solutions / 106

Fourteen: The Cultural Payoff / 122

Fifteen: Passing on the Baton / 129

Appendix: Remembering Boss / 133

Acknowledgements / 149

FOREWORD

Culture Eats Creativity for Lunch by Arvind Wable provides an insider's look at one of India's most innovative companies and how it achieved extraordinary success. Primarily, it not only tells the story of a firm that enjoyed dramatic success from the outset but also describes the ways in which new leadership changed the culture of the company to create a phoenix—a resurrected company that was far better than it was before.

The key to the dramatic success and turnaround of FCB Ulka was its management, leadership and organizational culture. Whereas many books have appeared on organizational success in India, very few, if any, focus on culture specifically and how to build a strong and positive culture. An in-depth description of the ways in which a new leadership team set about to create a new corporate culture makes for fascinating and informative reading. This team led the agency for the next 25 years and realized exceptional results.

This unique book illustrates in a captivating way the findings that have emerged from my own empirical research over the last several decades. These findings show how crucial organizational culture is in producing successful outcomes. The trouble is that it is difficult to define and recognize the elements of culture—what culture is, how to measure it and how to manage it. Arvind describes the usefulness of the frequently implemented approach to measuring and managing organizational culture in the world, namely, the Competing Values Framework. One chapter is dedicated to the question of how to measure and manage culture, and the analysis will be helpful to readers who are interested in culture change. More importantly, the book is a warm, highly readable and delightful illustration of how to create dramatic culture change, from an insider's view.

—Kim Cameron
Professor Emeritus of Management and Organizations, Ross School of Business, University of Michigan

INTRODUCTION

Culture eats creativity for lunch!

Coming from someone who spent most of his career in advertising, that seems an odd and incongruous statement. Very much like the statement by Peter Drucker: 'Culture eats strategy for breakfast'. Both the above statements do not intend to undermine the significance of creativity or strategy but are essentially bringing focus to culture as a critical ingredient for organizational success.

Culture, unfortunately, is an underrated factor in an organization's performance, whereas it is really the binding force that holds strategy, creativity, leadership and all other factors together.

The contention is that while creativity or innovation is a necessary ingredient in organizational performance, it is not sufficient to provide long-term sustainable growth. There are numerous examples of advertising agencies that were the flavour of the season due to their sole focus on creativity in the form of award-winning campaigns, which performed well for a few years, but then lost steam and fizzled out. As someone has said, 'Creativity without a clear strategy is just "art", whereas creativity based on a clearly defined strategy is "advertising".'

Then, the next question is what is culture? There are numerous definitions of culture, but the one thing they all have in common is that culture is the underlying way an organization works. It is the unwritten norms, values and behaviours that define and guide the day-to-day functioning of an organization, both internally and with respect to external entities and factors.

Studies have shown that a well-defined positive culture is the most critical ingredient of organizational success. But culture does not evolve in isolation nor is there one best kind of culture. Culture is the result of deliberate action over time and is a cultivated outcome of leadership styles. Culture needs constant nourishment to take root and to be kept alive and relevant through day-to-day practices, rituals, symbols, structures, rewards and strictures. This is why culture is intrinsically linked to leadership.

The other critical linkage of culture is strategy. Strategy is a plan evolved from the mix of consumer insights, competitive advantages and market environment to achieve certain designated goals while culture is a mix of values, beliefs, mindsets and social norms. Thus, culture enables the execution of strategies by equipping people within the organization with the right mindset and a unifying belief.

In cases where organizational culture and strategy are aligned, the beneficial outcomes are significantly higher than in organizations where there is a misalignment. When the leadership, culture and strategy are in sync with each other, we achieve the 'Goldilocks Zone'.[1]

There have been a lot of books on organizational success in India, but not many, if any, focus on culture. In fact, the

---

[1] The 'Goldilocks Zone' for an organization is the not-too-hot-not-too-cold space between extremes that will help it balance out the tensions that arise during growth. Harris, Brad, 'The Goldilocks Zone of High-Growth Organizations', *TrailHead*, 30 March 2022, https://www.teamtrailhead.com/insights/goldilocks-zone-of-high-growth-organizations.

reference material on organizational culture in the Indian context is pretty sparse. The focus of companies is largely on leadership, strategy, innovation, creativity, technologies and, more recently, on the importance of human capital, but very few focus on building a strong and positive culture, and even fewer see the link between leadership, strategy and culture.

A significant proportion of companies today believe that it is imperative to build high-pressure, result-oriented, competitive internal environments to achieve success. However, research is increasingly showing that the above is harmful to productivity over time and that building a strong and positive culture results in delivering substantially more beneficial outcomes in every aspect of the company's functioning, including profitability.[2] This is being realized all over the world, both by large established companies as well as start-ups.

Furthermore, culture is not constant. As the environment, markets and consumers change, the culture, strategy and even leadership need to adapt or change.

To understand culture at a conceptual level, I have used one of the most seminal models—the Competing Values Framework. The Competing Values Framework was developed based on studies on organizational effectiveness[3] and subsequent work on culture, leadership and organization structures.[4]

---

[2] Kumar, Sanjeev, Rahul Raj, Irfaan Salem, Etinder Pal Singh, Kavita Goel, and Rishi Bhatia, 'The Interplay of Organisational Culture, Transformational Leadership and Organisation Innovativeness: Evidence from India', *Asian Business & Management*, 2023, https://doi.org/10.1057/s41291-023-00230-9.

[3] Quinn, Robert E., and John Rohrbaugh, 'A Competing Values Approach to Organizational Effectiveness', *Public Productivity Review*, Vol. 5, No. 2, 1981, 122–40, https://doi.org/10.2307/3380029.

[4] Cameron, Kim S., and Robert E. Quinn, *Diagnosing and Changing Organizational Culture: Based on the Competing Values Framework (Third Edition)*, Jossey-Bass, San Francisco, CA, 15 April 2011.

The Competing Values Framework suggests four principal cultures: hierarchy culture, where the orientation of the organization is to control; clan culture, where the orientation of the organization is to collaborate; adhocracy culture, with an orientation to create; and market culture, where the orientation of the organization is to compete.

To illustrate all the above conceptual aspects of culture and the need to adapt, modify or change the culture with changing times, I have used the experience of Ulka Advertising (now FCB Ulka), one of the most successful and top advertising agencies in India.

The Ulka journey in the early years was like that of any start-up (at a time when it was a mere concept). A small group of talented people with a common vision, who were hungry for recognition and highly motivated, came together and started an agency in 1961. The team did phenomenal work—building brands, pushing breakthrough ideas, doing new things (a new typeface) and creating edgy illustrative designs and logos for some of today's big brands like the Welcome Group of Hotels, Punjab National Bank, etc. The intention was to be spontaneous and innovative. The culture was typically adhocracy with an aim to create.

Over the next two decades, Ulka grew rapidly and became an established mainline agency, with a larger team and multiple offices. The culture too shifted from being innovation-focused to more achievement- and result-oriented. It also became more internally competitive, with each office wanting to outdo other offices. The performance parameters and reward systems also changed accordingly. Hence, while the agency grew and prospered, the binding force of a common culture of the early years became weaker, and as a result the leadership, strategy and culture no longer aligned. This misalignment led to different offices creating their own subcultures and ultimately breaking away to start separate agencies. This transition compelled the founder directors to bring in a new leadership team to consolidate the various offices and set a different direction for future growth.

The new leadership took over in 1987–88 and had the unique distinction of having professionals equipped with an MBA (Master's in Business Administration) from one of the IIMs (Indian Institutes of Management), all of whom had worked in advertising and marketing before joining Ulka. This team came in with a unique marketing perspective on advertising and with a common vision to redefine the role of the agency, as not only designers of creative campaigns but also creators of brand solutions. However, the most significant challenge for the team was probably to set about building a culture that was collaborative and not competitive; a culture that was team-based rather than individual-based. This team led Ulka for the next 25 years, taking the agency to a high point as one of the top three advertising agency groups in India.

Between 2011 and 2015 another transition happened with the old guard moving on to advisory positions and handing over the agency leadership role to a younger group. With this leadership change came a modification of strategy and culture to suit the needs of the current market situation. This change in direction amalgamated the strategy orientation of the last 25 years with award-winning campaigns, with Ulka becoming the hottest creative agency with a slew of Cannes Lions and Clios. This ability to adapt its culture to a changing environment has once again put the agency on a path of growth.

Ulka is probably one of the few independent agency brands out of the many born in the 1960s that has prospered and survived to retain its large mainline agency group status for 60 years.

The focus of *Culture Eats Creativity for Lunch* is not on the achievements of the Ulka brand but more on its culture, with specific attention to the years between 1990 and 2011.

My motivation to write this book is to call attention to the importance of culture as a critical component in the success of organizations, and the benefits of the synergy that come with the alignment of leadership, strategy and culture.

I hope that the Ulka story, even though it is a decade old, will exemplify the relevance of culture as the most critical component of the success mantra in today's fast-changing, competitive world.

I believe that this book will be of interest to those who are keen enthusiasts of organizational culture in the Indian context. It will be relevant to those in the service, technology and fast-growing service delivery industries. Finally, it could help generate discussions or case studies in academic institutions and motivate them to create course material on organizational culture.

Culture Eats Creativity for Lunch is organized into 15 chapters. The first chapter is about the early years of Ulka, its inception and its success. The second chapter is about the changing environment, with the first stages of economic liberalization in India and its impact on the role of advertising agencies, including Ulka. The third chapter is about the coming in of a new management team and the formulation of the new strategic direction for Ulka, resulting in sustained growth over the next 20 years.

The fourth chapter is about the new vision, which was the underlying force for the agency in the two decades from 1990 to 2010, a period in which the new leadership, strategic direction and culture came together—the 'Goldilocks Zone'. This chapter also outlines the six major attributes of the Ulka culture or the *Ulkaway*.

The fifth to tenth chapters elaborate on the above key attributes of the Ulkaway while the eleventh chapter assimilates the attributes into a culture style using the Competitive Values Framework.

The twelfth chapter deals with the key question of strategy versus creativity as the driving force for Ulka with a couple of case stories. The thirteenth chapter exemplifies the positioning of Ulka as a creator of brand solutions and not only a supplier of creative campaigns. The fourteenth chapter highlights the relevance of the Ulka story in today's context and the tangible payoffs of a strong and positive culture. The fifteenth chapter is about the transition to a new leadership that is currently taking the agency into the future.

The appendix is a tribute to Anil Kapoor, who led the Ulka team and was the chief architect of the Ulka vision.

ONE

THE BEGINNING

Advertising is like a clear night sky filled with millions of stars that all look beautiful but alike. It is that one shooting star that streaks across the sky, standing out among the millions of very seemingly identical stars. It is a sight we never tire of and look forward to seeing again and again. Good advertising is like that shooting star.

The agency was named 'Ulka', the Sanskrit word for a shooting star, and the logo aptly had a star in it.

The above analogy and inspiration for the name 'Ulka' suddenly came to Bal Mundkur, the founder of the agency, when he went to his mother to seek her blessings before starting his agency.

On New Year's Day of 1961, an advertising agency was born. Unlike many other similar start-ups during that era, the agency was not named after its founders; instead, it was based on a vision of building Indian brands that could compete with the few but strongly entrenched multinational brands.

Ulka was founded by Bal Mundkur along with Ann Mundkur (now Ann Mukherjee) and a team of seven, including the legendary art director R.K. Joshi. Bal had been working at D.J. Keymer (now Ogilvy & Mather [O&M]) for over 10 years before starting his own agency. Bal's brother Bhaskar Mundkur, who was at Hindustan Lever Limited (HLL), also joined the agency shortly thereafter. From its very inception, Ulka focused on providing professional brand-building inputs to the emerging Indian business houses that were, for the first time, hoping to go beyond trading in commodities and being small-scale enterprises to become industrialists with a national footprint.

Indian family businesses like Birlas, Tatas, Godrejs, Thapars, Shrirams, Anands, Singhanias, Wadias, Sundarams, etc., all began diversifying their business interests. Simultaneously, the government, through large public sector companies, such as HMT Limited and the India Tourism Development Corporation (ITDC), also entered the consumer products/services arena. While the Licence Raj restricted competition, the low penetrations of almost every consumer product provided an attractive opportunity. The role of an advertising agency was pre-eminent among corporate partnerships, and to their credit, groundbreaking work was done during this period. Young Indian companies needed corporate identities, brand identities and professional marketing inputs to grow into new categories. In contrast, the government needed to promote welfare programmes such as the Integrated Child Development Services (ICDS) scheme, primary health centres, national family planning programme, etc., requiring large-scale promotional efforts in rural areas. Consumer product companies sought brand-building campaigns for soaps, shampoos, textiles, over-the-counter products, packaged foods, etc. Even today, many people can recall the early brands and their memorable advertising campaigns from 50 years ago. Brands like Amul, Bombay Dyeing, Hamam, Lux Soap and Bajaj Scooters are considered legendary in this regard.

Ulka also contributed to this indigenous effort by creating the early corporate identities for companies like SAIL (Steel Authority of India Limited), Crompton Greaves, Punjab National Bank, Gabriel and ITC Hotels, among many others.

Over the next decade, Ulka emerged as a creative boutique, working with Indian brands based on insights into Indian consumers rather than adapting campaigns of multinational brands for the local markets. The campaigns for Gabriel Shock Absorbers, Mukund Steel, Bombay Dyeing, Usha sewing machines and Safari luggage in the 1960s and early 1970s laid the foundations for the success of these brands in the years to come. The corporate campaign for ITC Limited was a precursor to the distinctively Indian ethos of ITC's hotel division. Zodiac was one of the first apparel brands to create a brand icon—the 'Zodiac Man'. In the social area, seminal campaigns for the government's family planning programme—the ICDS—added to the diverse portfolio of work.

By the early 1980s, Ulka was among the top 10 agencies with an impressive list of clients and probably the largest network of offices in the industry—Bombay (now Mumbai) and Calcutta (now Kolkata) in 1965, Delhi in 1971, Bangalore (now Bengaluru) in 1981, Hyderabad and Cochin (now Kochi) in 1985 and finally Madras (now Chennai) in 1989. The agency retained almost all its early relationships and added new ones, including Nerolac Paints, CEAT Tyres, Voltas, Godrej and Hero Honda, to its roster of clients. Having started as a boutique agency, it transformed into a mainline agency, poised for unfettered growth. Or so it hoped.

TWO

RISE, FALL, RESURRECTION

'Every institution, no matter how great, is vulnerable to decline. […] Anyone can fall and most eventually do. But […] decline, it turns out, is largely self-inflicted, and the path to recovery lies largely within our own hands. We are not imprisoned by our circumstances, our history, or even our staggering defeats along the way. As long as we never get entirely knocked out of the game, hope always remains. The mighty can fall, but they can often rise again.'

—Jim Collins

The economic liberalization of the late 1980s opened up the Indian economy to global trade. The introduction of TV as a medium sowed the seeds of consumerism, and advertising underwent a significant transformation in form, content and tonality. No longer confined to beautifully crafted English copy meant for the select, discerning, upmarket English-speaking audiences, advertising became democratized, Indian and mass-oriented. It reflected the upbeat mood and confidence of the emerging new consumer. Notable campaigns like 'Mile Sur Mera Tumhara'[5] captured this new spirit, embodying the evolving face of Indian advertising.

Over the next decade, the creative bar was raised and the Indian audience embraced advertising as much as TV programming. The buoyant financial markets and the first dotcom wave gave a further fillip to advertising and creativity. Global brands entering the Indian market led international agencies to take an interest in their Indian operations, with J. Walter Thompson (JWT), O&M and McCann Ericson acquiring controlling stakes in their Indian companies. Meanwhile, Leo Burnett, Publics and Young & Rubicam (Y&R) also invested in local agencies.

The role of the agencies and their relationship with client companies evolved with the opening up of the economy. In the 1960s and 1970s, the agencies' role of creating corporate and brand identities and the initial brand-building efforts meant a close relationship at the chairman and CEO levels and a greater influence of the agency on the client's overall marketing/sales strategy. However, by the early 1990s, with corporates diversifying and raising funds from a growing equity market, the agency's partnership with the senior management at the client's organization was diffused and replaced by other financial and management consultants/partners. Agencies, therefore, became more focused on dealing with marketing departments and, in many cases, down the line with brand managers.

This period also witnessed economic activity spreading across the country beyond the traditional commercial centres. The shift of large advertisers such as Britannia and Lipton to Bangalore, along with ITC's foray into consumer

---

[5]Mile Sur Mera Tumhara, YouTube, https://www.youtube.com/watch?v=JKueG7SnuWk.

products, provided an impetus to the southern markets. Liberalization also attracted multinational companies such as LG Electronics, Samsung, Panasonic and Coca-Cola, which established operations in Delhi, providing a massive boost to the advertising market in the national capital.

While Bombay remained the dominant centre for advertising, growth became more evenly spread across other cities. Ulka, with a widespread network of offices in the four metros and in cities like Bangalore, Hyderabad and Cochin, was well placed to capitalize on this growth. This success attracted some of the best talent during this phase and, as a result, the agency produced remarkable advertising for brands like Bombay Dyeing, Hero Honda, ICI, Duncan's Tea, Uptron, etc. In rapidly growing markets like Delhi, Ulka was almost vying for the top slot with established players like Hindustan Thompson Associates (HTA, till recently JWT), which had held a dominant position in the market for decades.

My association with Ulka began in 1987–88 when I served as the general manager of marketing at UDI Yellow Pages [United Database (India) Pvt. Ltd.]. Prior to joining UDI, I had spent four productive years at Network Communications, a Hindustan Computers Pvt. Limited (HCL) group start-up. Anil Kapoor and Ambi Parameswaran, both of whom had recently departed from Boots, persuaded me to join them in launching India's first Yellow Pages. I had known Anil for a long time and Ambi was a client at Boots when I was at HTA Bombay.

UDI was introducing the Yellow Pages in India alongside the telephone directory (white pages) for Mahanagar Telephone

Nigam Limited (MTNL) in Delhi, Bombay and Calcutta. This required collating, printing and distributing over 1.7 million directories for the three cities within six months, free of charge. UDI had to generate revenue by marketing the Yellow Pages—a daunting task—especially considering that telephone directories were traditionally printed once every three or four years and the concept of Yellow Pages was unfamiliar in India. During my two years at UDI, from 1987 to 1988, we recruited, trained and deployed a team of over 300 young individuals, establishing one of the first large telemarketing operations in the country. The team did a phenomenal job selling a whole new concept of Yellow Pages, resulting in over 1.7 million sets of telephone directories and Yellow Pages being collated, printed and delivered on schedule. To achieve this, we needed an agency partner capable of breakthrough work and supporting us in all three metros to market this new concept to telephone subscribers. After an extensive agency search, we chose Ulka as our partner.

With offices in eight cities and the launch of a second agency, Interface, the Ulka group had the largest advertising agency network in the country and, as expected, added significantly to its revenue and profits.

However, this rapid growth came at the cost of the cohesive spirit that characterized the early years. New-found success created new power centres with their own subcultures, diluting the shared values that were the hallmarks of the formative years. This resulted in the creation of mini-empires within the organization, with each office developing its own culture and, in some cases, competing with offices in other cities.

The Delhi agency team fell apart in 1988 when the office head left to form a new agency along with 30 people. The solid old client relationships got strained and several clients started reviewing their association with the agency. Ulka began losing people and clients rapidly, resulting in declining revenues and depleting bottom lines. UDI also parted ways with Ulka and I appointed Contract Advertising as my new agency partner.

The founding team, which had steered the agency admirably for the previous 25 years, was fatigued and eager to sell their stakes and call it a day. It was time for a new leadership to take over the reins of the agency.

While Bal Mundkur remained the chairman and Ann Mukerjee the director, Anil Kapoor came in as the new managing director in August 1988.

THREE

BECOMING FCB ULKA

Ulka was established with the simple belief that the business of advertising has to be just that—business. The core principle is that when you build brands, you are creating real and tangible wealth for the future. So it's not merely about that clever line or a humorously self-indulgent commercial. The focus has never been on creating ads for awards or nurturing self-centred prima donnas. And more importantly, it's never been about hiding behind excuses. Because we are in the business of adding sheen not to our own but to the client's image. We are in the business of building brands in the present and contributing to brand value over time. Or building brand wealth, as we prefer to think of it.

The new leadership team took over the agency in 1988–89. The first few years were challenging, marked by a turnover of key personnel and strained client relationships. Consequently, the emphasis was on consolidating our position with existing clients, many of whom had strong ties with the earlier team. The market buzzed with rumours about which senior figures would stay, who was looking to move out and speculation about the potential closure of the Ulka Delhi office. Clients, too, were uncertain about the agency's service standards and the continuity of their key relationships.

In such circumstances, acquiring new business proved to be a formidable task. Invitations for pitches posed a challenge, as prospects were also aware of the internal changes in the agency. Therefore, we adopted a three-pronged approach to consolidate the existing clients. The first was to convince them of the commitment and the unique credentials of the new team in providing brand-building ideas. Second, we assured them that every major client would be personally handled by a member of the senior management team. Third, service standards would be maintained through a national pooling of resources, ensuring that work and timelines did not suffer. If one office lacked certain resources, another office would spare the resources to get the job done. With these strategies, we managed to retain almost all the major clients and launched some groundbreaking campaigns during the first few years for ICI, Usha, Zodiac, Voltas, Nerolac Paints and Amulya Dairy Whitener.

The first breakthroughs in new business came with the relaunch of Santoor soap for Wipro Consumer Care and the launch of Sundrop refined oil.

Despite resource pressures, we did not hire indiscriminately. We were very clear about the type of team we wanted to build and it had to be composed of the right individuals. Every person recruited during the first few years, from account executive to account director or copywriter to creative director, was carefully vetted for both their aptitude and, more importantly, their attitude. In cases where there was a gap in resources, we filled it either by doubling up or by having one of the other offices contribute their best talent.

By 1995–96, Ulka had carved out a unique and distinctive position as an agency with a difference, recognized in marketing circles for outstanding brand-building work, reviving old brands and successfully launching new ones. The agency had built an enviable portfolio, which included a number of case studies for repositioning brands like Santoor soap[6] and Sundrop refined oil[7] (1989); LML, Voltas washing machines, Usha sewing machines, Godrej Storwel (1991–92); Tropicana juices, Captain Cook atta (1993); the Doodh Doodh Doodh (Amul Milk) campaign for the National Dairy Development Board (1996); Escotel (1996); etc.

The success of these brand-building campaigns was measurable not only in terms of brand saliency and image but also in how significantly they contributed to increasing market share and the value added to the client's marketing efforts. Case studies for brands like LML, Sundrop, Santoor and Tropicana led to new business wins. In many cases, we secured new business based solely on credential presentations, showcasing the strategic value addition to the marketing efforts of these clients. We refused to present creative campaigns at the pitch stage. Our approach was very clear—we are not in the business of selling creative campaigns but of finding brand solutions and adding value to the client's marketing efforts. In many cases, we declined to present creative campaigns until the clients first agreed to the marketing or advertising strategy. Most often, the strategic inputs included not only a communication strategy but also product, price and distribution ideas.

The result was significant new business wins like Whirlpool and Tata Motors in 1997–98, propelling the agency to become

---

[6]Santoor Bookshop (1989–93), YouTube, https://www.youtube.com/watch?v=y2jHheBM0pk.
[7]Sundrop—Mom & Son (Cartwheel), YouTube, https://www.youtube.com/watch?v=dH71FBR6Q_I.

the preferred choice for marketers seeking holistic brand solutions.

During these years, the advertising industry underwent a change as a result of the Indian economy opening up and the entry of multinationals. This period also witnessed the fragmentation of the agency business, transitioning from a one-stop-shop model to specialized agencies for media planning, media buying, direct marketing, event marketing, etc. Ulka stood out as one of the few independent agencies to establish specialized divisions such as Lodestar (Media), Direct & Digital, Events and Procyon Production. Here again, there was the typical Ulka approach aimed at offering value addition to clients by providing integrated solutions through these specialized divisions. Unlike many agency groups that established separate financially independent units for each specialized area, often competing with the main agency for business, Ulka opted for a different approach by having these divisions under one bottom line. The client management and strategy teams effectively coordinated the services of all specialized divisions, eliminating the need for clients to brief and coordinate with each division separately.

While Ulka experienced accelerated growth as an independent agency, it lacked global alignments, missing out on opportunities with large and growing multinational clients who were increasingly working with globally aligned networks.

To address this, Ulka aligned with Foote, Cone & Belding (FCB), a prominent agency brand in the United States. Its 125-year heritage of brand-building for iconic names like Levi's, Colgate, Sunkist, Clairol, Coors, SC Johnson and a host of other legendary brands solidified our choice in favour of FCB. The acquisition process was completed by 1997 and the agency was rebranded as FCB Ulka.

Unlike other Indian agency brands acquired by global networks, we retained the Ulka name as FCB was a relatively lesser-known brand in India. While the FCB acquisition provided Ulka with a global connection, it unfortunately did not lead to significant global business as FCB lost key clients like Citibank, Colgate and Levi's over the next two years.

Hence, FCB Ulka had to rely on securing business locally, winning clients like Frito-Lay, Reckitt Benckiser, HP and Whirlpool through local pitches against globally aligned agencies.

In 2001, FCB was acquired by the Interpublic Group (IPG), the number one global communications group. Due to this takeover, Ulka was required to give up clients like Tropicana, Reckitt Benckiser and Frito-Lay owing to global conflicts with IPG businesses. Unfortunately, all of these were Delhi office clients, resulting in a significant revenue loss for the office and the agency.

During this period, one of the significant losses due to alignment conflict was the HP business. We had won HP in a pitch against the globally aligned agency Publicis, and over two years, it had grown into one of our largest businesses in the Delhi office. Unfortunately, we had to give it up as FCB had finally secured the global Compaq account. Despite making strong representations to the regional and global teams, urging them to allow Ulka to continue with both HP and the Compaq business—with the latter being a third the size of the HP business and proposed to be placed in our second agency, Interface—the powers that be did not agree to the suggestion. The irony is that within a year, HP acquired Compaq, resulting in the loss of both businesses. So much for the benefits of being a part of a global network!

Despite these setbacks, the agency continued to grow ahead of the industry curve and, more importantly, maintained a very healthy bottom line.

On 1 June 2006, FCB rebranded to Draftfcb and the Indian agency became Draftfcb Ulka. By this time, we had secured a significant global business SC Johnson (SCJ) located in Delhi. This was a wonderful opportunity for us, to finally be a part of the global network in a meaningful way, as SCJ was the largest account for Draftfcb. Meanwhile, the Indian agency continued on its growth path and gained recognition in the global network as one of the model offices, a sort of 'Jewel in the Crown', due to its stable leadership, strong client relationships and outstanding financial performance. This brought recognition to the India team, with Anil Kapoor being appointed regional head for Asia Pacific and South Africa, and receiving a nomination on the Worldwide Council. Many of us on the Indian leadership team were invited to join various global forums. Personally, I took on additional responsibility as the chief executive officer (CEO) of Draftfcb, Singapore.

It was a landmark year for Ulka in 2011 as the agency celebrated 50 years of its existence. It was a momentous occasion, considering that Ulka was one of the few Indian agency brands that had retained its identity after half a century and held a top-three agency group ranking.

On 1st February 2011, the agency celebrated its 50th anniversary. It was a nostalgic affair, with everyone who had ever worked at the agency invited to parties held across the country to relive old memories of clients, campaigns and characters who had scripted the five decades of the Ulka story.

While the usual paraphernalia of special supplements, press releases, exclusive interviews with global board members, client testimonials, Facebook pages, etc., were rolled out in keeping with the Ulka positioning, a new initiative called BrandWealth was launched.

BrandWealth was the agency's commitment to adding value to our clients in a tangible manner. A three-day integrated marketing workshop covering every aspect of brand strategy, from brand identity, brand positioning, insight mining, market research, creative strategy, creative appreciation, media planning to analytics, was launched. The workshop was conducted by the most senior people in the agency across the country. Clients and prospects sent mid-level managers and paid a nominal fee to cover the cost of the programme. The BrandWealth seminars became a huge success with over 120 participants in the first year across three cities and growing to over 250 participants across five cities by 2013.

Another significant outcome of the 50th-year celebrations was the goodwill it generated among past and present Ulkans, a name coined for all those who had ever worked in the agency. The constant refrain, especially by those who had been at the agency in the last twenty years, was the unique and distinctive culture of Ulka.

This was especially significant as, keeping in line with the agency's core values, the management team that took over Ulka in the late 1980s and had led it since was gradually moving on to non-executive positions over the next five years, creating opportunities for the next generation of leadership to take on active management roles. The current leadership team would remain involved as coaches and mentors, facilitating a smooth transition to a new leadership team poised to take the agency to greater heights of success in the future.

As the first to move on to a non-executive role as an advisor to the Board, I took on the task of documenting the evolution, consolidation and practice of the Ulka culture, or what I fondly call the *Ulkaway*.

FOUR

BUILT TO LAST

'Architects of visionary companies don't just trust in good intentions or "values statements"; they build cult-like cultures around their core ideologies.'

—Jim Collins

I n this chapter, I will take you back to 1987–89, a period marked by the transition to new leadership, as outlined in Chapter 2, and the early evolution and building of the critical pillars of the new Ulka—the leadership team, the structure, the strategy and the culture.

LEADERSHIP AND TEAM BUILDING

Anil's primary focus, as the team head and managing director, was on the nature and composition of the team that would provide leadership to the agency. Over a period of 15 months, the new management team emerged, with the exit of some of the old guard and the retention/elevation to senior positions of a few individuals who were aligned with the new vision.

The new leadership team was unique in many ways, particularly for an advertising agency. Each member of the leadership team was an MBA from one of the IIMs and all had prior experience in advertising, sales and marketing. Moreover, every team member had been a client of one or more of the top 10 agencies. As a group, the team possessed hands-on experience across a broad spectrum of industries/categories, ranging from pharmaceuticals to personal care products, beverages to banking and office automation to Yellow Pages marketing. Importantly, most of them had collaborated with each other at various points in their careers.

Anil Kapoor, the managing director, graduated from St. Stephen's College, Delhi, and earned an MBA from IIM Ahmedabad. Over the next 20 years, he built an enviable reputation in marketing and advertising. Starting his career at DCM Shriram, he moved to MCM Advertising and later joined Boots, where he led the company's marketing function for the next 15 years—the last five of which were spent as marketing director—before joining Ulka.

Anil set about to build a new leadership team and identified two individuals from the existing Ulka team—Niteen Bhagwat, the manager of Ulka Bombay, and Shashi Sinha, the strategic planning head. Niteen, also an alumnus of IIM Ahmedabad, had previous advertising experience at HTA and had served as a product manager and later as a branch manager at Lakme, India's leading cosmetics company, before joining Ulka. Shashi, a BTech graduate from IIT Kanpur and an MBA from IIM Bangalore, had worked as a product manager at Parle Agro Beverages, India's largest soft drink company, and later as a regional sales manager at Herbertsons, a liquor and beverage company.

The new inductee to the leadership team, apart from me, was M.G. Parameswaran (Ambi), a BTech from IIT Madras and MBA from IIM Calcutta, who had worked in advertising at Rediffusion (Y&R) and then at Boots, where he served as marketing manager, before joining UDI Yellow Pages as general manager of sales.

I joined Ulka in June 1989, having started my career in advertising at HTA, where Anil and Ambi were clients and Niteen was a colleague. My educational background includes a BA in Economics from St. Stephen's College, an MA in Economics from the Delhi School of Economics and an MBA from IIM Ahmedabad. My first job was at HTA Madras, working with one of the best advertising men I have known, the legendary Ram Ray. This was followed by four years in marketing at the highly successful start-up, Network Communications, where I served as the marketing manager, launching the first microprocessor-based electronic typewriters. My last assignment before Ulka was with Anil and Ambi as part of the founding team at another start-up UDI, where we launched the country's first-ever Yellow Pages.

The last to join the Ulka team was Nagesh Alai, the company CFO. A qualified lawyer, company secretary and cost accountant, he too had previously worked with Anil and Ambi at Boots, preceded by John Wyeth (now Wyeth BioPharma).

Ironically, just a year before joining the agency, I had recommended parting ways with Ulka when I was at UDI Yellow Pages. It's interesting to note that when Anil informed Bal about his plan to offer me the position of heading Ulka Delhi, Bal threw a fit, giving out his choicest! Nonetheless, Anil prevailed, and despite a frosty welcome note from Bal when I joined, we eventually developed a very cordial relationship over the years, which persisted even after his retirement and move to Goa.

The process of team-building for the Delhi office mirrored the challenges faced by the entire agency. I recall the early days at Ulka Delhi when there was a significant exodus of staff in response to the announcement of the new leadership. Many left due to the agency's poor performance, while others departed because they felt they identified with the old Ulka culture and disagreed with the changes that were happening at the agency. It came to a stage where there was not a single copywriter left within two weeks of my joining the Delhi office.

Most of the senior servicing team had either left before my arrival or were contemplating a change. Although the temptation to offer enticing deals to retain key individuals or hire anyone willing to join was strong, it did not feel like the right thing to do, even in the early days before the vision had fully been developed. It was no use having sceptics on the team. Instead, it seemed better to build a team from scratch, with committed individuals who understood and were aware of the challenges ahead. Despite the struggles facing the office and external perceptions of an agency in decline, those who were brave enough to join were individuals who had previously worked with me and believed in our vision.

My first senior hire was Nitish Mukherjee, who used to head the team at Contract, handling the UDI Yellow Pages business. I vividly remember our meeting over drinks at Le Meridian in Delhi, where Nitish, aware of the situation at Ulka, asked me what the team was going to be. My response was, 'As long as there are two of us, we are a team; the rest we will build as we go along.' For Nitish, joining Ulka was a leap of faith in me, I suppose. The next addition to the team was Richa Arora, who had previously worked at Contract on the UDI Yellow Pages account. In the early days, Radhika Handa (now Shapoorjee) and Archana Grover, both standout salespeople from UDI Yellow Pages, also joined Ulka. Rajiv Shukla, Sudhir Sahni, Sanjeev Bhargava and Roy Cherian joined over the next couple of years. Praveen Saxena came on board to handle language copy, while some of the long-standing creative team members, including Darsh Mehra, Deepak Bagga and Anil Manan, stayed on, providing stability to our operations. Vibha Desai, serving as media manager, and Santosh Desai, as the head of account planning, were part of the old team and stayed for about two years before moving on. Everyone who joined in those early years was a believer and was committed to the long haul. Senior team attrition was almost non-existent for the next five years, with most staying with the agency for a decade or more.

VALUES THAT BIND

Nitish Mukherjee recollects our first meeting and how he joined Ulka. Subsequently, he has gone on to become the managing director at Orchard Advertising and later at Leo Burnett. Currently, he serves as an advisor, coach and mentor. Nitish recalls:

Anil Kapoor, Ambi Parameswaran and Arvind Wable were colleagues at UDI Yellow Pages when I first met them. Our agency managed the account and I was the team lead. Arvind was my primary point of contact, and over a period of time we got to know each other quite well. So it wasn't really a surprise when, soon after joining Ulka Advertising, I received a call from him, enquiring if I could meet him at Le Meridian that evening.

I admired Arvind not only for his intelligence and professional competence but also for the person he was. Gracious and suave, he was a natural charmer and any opportunity to meet him was always welcome.

As I walked into the bar at Le Meridian that evening,

Arvind was already there, perched on a bar stool with one leg tucked under and the other stretched out. In front of him were two glasses of Bloody Mary. He spoke while gesturing me to the stool next to him, 'I decided to have the drinks ready so that we don't have to waste any time.' Bloody Mary was my favourite drink at the time and it felt good that he remembered. Before I could express my thanks, he made his next statement, 'I wanted to meet you today to tell you that I would like you to join me at Ulka.' I was really glad that the drinks were already lined up.

It was unexpected and I tried to gain time and gather myself by asking a flurry of questions. 'What position did you have in mind? Which businesses would I work on? How many people will be in my team?' Arvind looked me straight in the eye and said, 'Nitish, things are not good. I am literally losing one account a week and a person a day as we speak. You probably have a notice period of two months. By the time you come in, it is difficult to say how much or what will be there.' He took a long pause, stared at his outstretched foot for a while, then looked up and continued, 'But I do know one thing ... if I have one good person by my side and one client, we will build this back to one of the finest offices. We can't offer much today. You can share your current salary, and I will try to match that for now, but I will make sure that you don't regret coming on board.'

I must admit that I did think that only a madman could make such an offer, but the madness was probably infectious as well because before the drink was over, I had said yes to joining Ulka. We agreed to meet next week so that he could give me my appointment letter. What the offer would be was still unknown to both of us.

We met over lunch the following week at the coffee shop at

The Imperial, Janpath. They had an excellent Shepherd's Pie and I was about to finish mine while occasionally eyeing the manilla envelope lying next to Arvind when he finally said, 'I have your appointment letter right here Nitish. It arrived just this morning but I can't give it to you. I have to send it back to Bombay for changes. As is the normal procedure, they have mentioned a probation period of six months in the letter. I don't think it is fair in our scheme of things for that to be included in your letter. I understand this means a further delay for you in putting in your papers and therefore, the date when you can join us; we will have to live with that.' However, when I explained that he needn't worry about my joining date as I had already put in my resignation the day after I met him, the look of surprise on Arvind's face was palpable. To his query, 'What made you put in your papers without an appointment letter in your hand?', pat came my reply, 'You seemed to be in a hurry.'

This kernel of trust was one of the endearing values that I experienced and lived with for over a decade at Ulka. That trust manifested itself in many ways in the company and its sphere of influence. It built strong teams, great relationships with clients as well as business associates, and an edifice of sustainable and profitable growth over many years. It wasn't infallible; it had its fault lines, but the undeniable quest to create, cherish and honour trust was one of the hallmarks of the Ulka I knew.

THE STRUCTURE

For the team to work as a cohesive unit, it was critical to establish a management structure that encouraged a collaborative mindset for executing the day-to-day operations. While fostering an entrepreneurial spirit and a sense of ownership and freedom in each business head was important, working towards a common purpose was equally, if not more, vital. The aim was to cultivate a sense of camaraderie—a kind of Musketeer's bond—where a 'one for all, all for one' spirit prevailed. Consequently, a matrix structure evolved that ensured that everyone on the leadership team was interdependent in achieving both their individual goals and the collective team goals.

While Ambi, Shashi and Niteen shared the responsibility for the flagship Mumbai office business, they were also assigned additional roles. Ambi took charge of the southern offices and strategic planning, Shashi managed HR, media and the Calcutta office while Niteen handled technology. My responsibilities included Delhi, Lucknow and Interface (our second agency). Nagesh held the critical finance portfolio.

THE STRATEGY

An excellent understanding of the marketing environment in the early 1990s was essential to actualize the strategy of positioning Ulka as also a creator of brand solutions rather than only a supplier of creatives.

During this period, two prevailing agency success models emerged. One involved creating clutter-busting creative campaigns for the mushrooming dot-com sector and the newly liberalized financial sector and equity market—both of which were looking for quick, high-saliency campaigns for visibility and valuation with no long-term brand-building expected.

While this might have been an expedient option for Ulka to boost its sagging bottom line and profile, it was clear to the new team that this would be a trap. This approach could lead the agency into a groove that would be challenging to escape once the boom ended. Moreover, it lacked differentiation, as many other agencies were on the same bandwagon. The boom eventually went bust in the next few years, leaving numerous agencies with overextended overheads and massive unpaid bills from upstart clients who either went bust or struggled to secure valuation and funding.

The other engine for sustained growth for many mainline agencies was globally aligned business with major advertisers like HLL, Colgate, Nestle, Pepsi and Coke. These advertisers, investing in the Indian market, increasingly consolidated their business with their global agency partners such as JWT, O&M, Leo Burnett, McCann, etc. As an independent agency, Ulka did not have the crutch of a globally aligned business and had to rely on Indian companies.

Ulka saw the opportunity to fill a gap left by the advertising industry vacating the marketing/brand consultant position they had once occupied. The objective was to enhance the old model by providing a solid marketing orientation to Indian advertising.

In the prevailing scenario, sustainable brand-building work was driven by enlightened, marketing-oriented clients with minimal agency inputs. Hence, positioning the agency as a brand consultancy offering end-to-end brand solutions was no easy task. In fact, the challenge was heightened by the entry of MBAs from the IIMs and other top-grade business schools into marketing over the previous two decades. Unlike their predecessors, these individuals considered themselves well equipped with modern marketing methods and brand-building strategies. Their expectations from the agency were limited to providing a creative interpretation of the client brief.

To be able to change perceptions and the agency's role, Ulka had to match, if not surpass, the marketing talent available at the client's end. The goal was to provide value-added brand solutions to meet marketing objectives in a tangible, measurable manner. The detailed outcomes of this strategy are outlined in Chapter 12, which discusses 'Strategy vs Creativity', and Chapter 13, which delves into 'Creating Brand Solutions', presented in the form of case stories.

THE VISION

The fourth pillar of the vision aimed to instil a new mindset and a set of values that would foster a fresh agency culture. Crucially, this change in mindset needed to originate from the top leadership and permeate throughout the entire agency. This proved to be the most challenging yet arguably the critical aspect of executing the vision. The leadership team had to fully embrace the new value system before transmitting it to the rest of the agency. Furthermore, the vision and values were not intended to become gilt-edged documents or mere plaques adorning boardroom walls; the idea was to practise the values in the day-to-day decisions. Hence, every aspect of the new value system was debated ad nauseam by the management board. Anil Kapoor's forceful personality and tireless commitment to discussing any issue until achieving the consensus of the entire leadership team led to the development of the Ulkaway code. Anil adhered to the axiom that 'organizational culture is the result of deliberate action, not of spontaneous tradition'.

In the early years, many of these new values seemed to be at odds with the accepted norms of behaviour in the industry. The management board would spend hours and days discussing what seemed like the most mundane issues to ensure our actions were aligned with the value codes we had established. There were numerous occasions when the values being discussed seemed like mere rhetoric. However, as the years passed and 'the preach became the practice', these commandments evolved into guiding principles for the agency. Many times, this meant forgoing short-term gains and resisting expedient measures to stay consistent with the value system. This is crucial because if the organizational culture is not in sync with the organization's strategy, it can derail even the best-laid plans. On the contrary, when the two are in sync, they become a force multiplier.

The coming together of Ulka's strategy, which emphasized brand solutions over mere creative campaigns, coupled with a culture of collaboration and interdependence forming the basis for all interactions within the organization and with the external environment, alongside a senior team practising the shared values and strategic vision in day-to-day work became the success mantra for the agency.

ATTRIBUTES OF THE ULKAWAY

What made up the Ulkaway? Before we get into the specifics, it is important to understand the concept of culture.

Culture serves as the implicit binding force within an organization, comprising elements such as Values & Beliefs, Symbols & Rituals, Motivations & Mindsets and Shared Assumptions. It dictates how individuals interact and respond to situations within the organization, residing in the informal, unwritten norms of accepted behaviour. It embodies the soft power of the organization.

The next six chapters explore the attributes of the Ulkaway, guiding the agency in its day-to-day work, recruitment, retention, promotion and decision-making processes.

1. Attitude vs Aptitude
2. Advertising Is a Senior Person's Business
3. Never Buy People
4. Prima Donnas
5. No Zero No Hero Overnight
6. No Turf Wars

These chapters encapsulate the essence of the Ulkaway and represent the values our team cultivated and practised for over two decades. What made the Ulkaway distinctive and unique was the fact that many of these values defied the accepted norms in the advertising industry. In the following chapters, I have tried to explain and elaborate on how these attributes of culture were practised. The anecdotes and experiences of various individuals who were a part of the Ulka journey add a unique flavour to the culture story.

FIVE

ATTITUDE VS APTITUDE

'Your attitude, not your aptitude, will determine your altitude.'

—Zig Ziglar

One of the most pivotal factors in building a strong and positive organizational culture is the mindset of individuals—their attitude towards work, relationships and life in general. Although there exists no exact measure for attitude, nor a predefined set of factors to determine it, at Ulka, we developed a set of criteria that we followed consistently over the years when recruiting individuals at all levels.

This process of instilling the right attitude started with our management training (MT) programme. The objective was to nurture a group of young professionals from business and art schools who would form the bulwark of the talent base in the years ahead. In addition to reinforcing the consultancy positioning of the agency through business school backgrounds, an equally significant objective of the MT programme was to inculcate the right value systems (attitude) at the outset. Given that most of the hires in the MT programme had no previous professional experience, they brought with them fresh perspectives, devoid of preconceived ideas or hardened attitudes. The early entrants hailed from the finest business schools in the country, including the prestigious IIMs. Consequently, there was an ever-growing pool of talent within the agency, both at the upper and entry levels, comprising the right aptitude and, more importantly, aligning with the core values of Ulka. Branded as Star One, the MT programme became the longest-running and most sought-after initiative in the advertising industry.

We identified several key attributes that we were looking for when assessing the attitude of the individual.

BELIEVERS VS SCEPTICS

The clear objective was to build an army of believers because mercenaries never win wars. We often cite the Vietnam War as one of the finest examples of this, where a handful of people in straw hats and bamboo sticks took on the might of the greatest military force in the world. The crucial difference lay in the belief of the Vietnamese people, as opposed to the lack of it among the American soldiers who had no understanding or belief in the war. They were fighting someone else's war, on someone else's soil, to defend someone else's freedom. Hence, the belief in the vision of the agency became ingrained in each one of us. This was achieved more through practical actions than mere preaching.

Whether it was the Star One programme, running year after year irrespective of economic cycles; the annual appraisal system; or the policies regarding increment and promotion, the underlying theme was one of nurturing, warmth and fairness within the organization, coupled with the integrity of advice for clients. In subsequent years, this approach continued with initiatives such as the partnership programme and the emphasis on internal growth.

THE ADVERTISING PERSONALITY

Interest and passion for the business are rooted in a specific mindset—the ability to enjoy the process as much as the end result. Unlike many roles in marketing and sales that become repetitive over time, in advertising, every day and every job brings something new. You do not replicate the same ad ever again, with the exception of tender notices, of course! However, the advertising process can be frustrating for those unaccustomed to long hours, relatively lower pay in the initial stages and, of course, the constant, often impossible, deadlines. Most client briefs arrive at five-thirty in the evening, especially on Fridays, with the expectation that the agency will revert with new creative ideas by Monday morning. It's important to develop a philosophical attitude towards the process of creation, rejection, re-creation and fresh creation, which characterizes agency life. Ideas believed to be brilliant by the agency are often rejected by clients, requiring the ability to pick oneself up again and either work on a new idea or represent the old idea more convincingly—necessitating a certain attitude. This requires an understanding that there will be good days and bad days, wins and losses and the development of a certain detachment to these ups and downs, learning from each experience.

I recall my early days at JWT as a young account executive. I worked with a client to whom I presented over three dozen layouts for a print ad over a one-year period. Each option was different from the earlier ones presented, yet none were approved. I passed on the legacy to the next account executive when I moved on to another business but left with a lot of goodwill from my client.

There were other clients that required multiple campaigns every year. The ability to enjoy the process as well as the result is a critical trait in a good advertising professional. Over the years, this attitude of 'win some, lose some' helped me deal with the successes and failures that came my way, enabling me to lift my team out of low periods of business or the frustration that set in when, despite prolonged agency efforts, the client would not approve a campaign or kept changing their minds or the briefs.

A vivid memory of an experience from my early days at Ulka involved one of the oldest clients for Ulka Delhi. Within weeks of my taking over the Delhi office, we were to present the next year's campaign. I wanted to review the work done so far and the team came with literally a bag full of alternative campaigns. The only way to see them together was to lay them out on the carpet in my room. The work done over the last six months covered the entire floor. Every possible layout, headline and visual combination had been tried and all had been rejected by the client. The creative team had given up and refused to continue creating more options.

This is when I remembered a piece of advice from one of my ex-bosses many years ago, 'When a client brief is not working, recreate the brief.' So I asked the team to stop all work on the client brief and create our own brief. This broke the cycle of creation, rejection and re-creation, and we came up with a totally different approach, distinct from the client's original brief but meeting their larger marketing objectives. We presented it to the client and it worked wonders. I have discussed this experience in detail in the Usha case story in Chapter 12.

LONERS DO NOT MAKE GOOD TEAMMATES

You need team players who pass the ball to those in a better position to score the goal. Loners tend not to share; even the most gifted can be self-obsessed. While individually brilliant, they often have the potential to pull down the entire team. At Ulka, our stance was crystal clear—we sought team players. While team leaders had a say in selecting their teams, they were also tasked with creating a cohesive unit.

While discussion, debate and different opinions were encouraged, once the team decided on a certain approach, everyone else was expected to fall in line. Ideas were freely shared and suggestions to improve upon an idea were valued and not set aside just because they came from someone other than the one who originally shared the idea.

AMICABLE VS OFFICIOUS

Despite their ever-growing hierarchies, agencies, at an operational level, function as a classless society. Therefore, early in one's agency life it is important to get to know and earn the respect of everyone in the system—from the dispatcher to the artist in the studio, from the receptionist to the pre-production head, from the admin manager to the creative director or, for that matter, from the accountant to the strategic planner. While advertising revolves around insights and ideas, in the ultimate analysis it is the ability to navigate through the agency system that results in flawless execution. In all these interactions what matters most is your attitude towards work and people, not just how bright you are.

This lesson became evident to me early in my career as an account executive working on accounts like Air India and Bombay Dyeing. The Air India hoardings at Nariman Point and Kemps Corner required fresh designs almost every week. This demanded a continuous flow of briefs, creative ideas, client approval and execution. It was my responsibility to ensure that this entire system worked flawlessly. I would receive the brief from Ruby Davar or Uttara Parikh at Air India, rush back to the office, convert it to a creative brief format and then coax David Innes, the copywriter, to start working on it. Simultaneously, I needed to coordinate with Sawant, the art director, to hand-paint the designs, follow up with Rui Menezes, the studio manager, to assign an artist for the lettering and paste-up, have it approved by Shiela or Ivan Arthur and then rush to Air India for approval from Mr Dabholkar, the Air India publicity boss, and pray that he does not reject our suggestion. Finally, I had to ensure that the design reached the hoarding painter, who lived in Juhu, and hope that he was not in an alcoholic haze and would put up the scaffolding and paint the hoarding at night, ready for the world to see next morning. All this used to happen over two days.

At Ulka, this early learning translated into a ritual. Almost every day of my 26 years at Ulka, the first thing I would do upon entering the office was to take a walk to every department—from billing, production, studio, creative to client servicing—meeting and chatting with people, sharing a joke, enquiring about their families or simply greeting them. This created personal relations with each one of them and a lasting bond that stood the test of time, especially when things were difficult and I needed to push the team or make tough decisions.

WHAT'S IN IT FOR ME?

'What have you done for me lately?'
'What can you potentially do for me next week?'
'If I do this, what will I get?'

'If I say this, will you do this for me?'

This attitude serves as a strong driving force for many people and numerous organizations encourage it because they believe that it gets the best out of their team. However, at Ulka, we held a different perspective—an entrepreneurial spirit persisted, even though no one on the board held a single share in the company.

We fostered a 'one for all, all for one' attitude. While each person had individual responsibilities, there were no turf issues. Offices readily assisted each other, often stretching their own resources. This approach was adopted at the very top and permeated through the organization. While individual performance was recognized, the emphasis was always on applauding the team. Growth and rewards were linked to consistent performance over time; there was no hero no zero overnight. A person's approach to work was deemed as important as the results achieved.

COLLABORATIVE VS COMPETITIVE

The most commonly held belief is that competition encourages the best to come forth; it drives excellence and innovation. However, if unchecked, it can also encourage internal rivalry and act as an antidote to team spirit. Many agencies thrive on a competitive culture, especially in creative fields, with each person or team zealously guarding their ideas and sometimes working to undermine others to secure a victory. At Ulka, we have always preferred a collaborative effort as it promotes team building, synergy and a stress-free, sharing environment. The matrix structure at senior levels and in large creative teams (rather than creative partners) resulted in the creation of an internal structure that aided collaboration. Strategic insights and creative ideas were discussed in common groups and more than one creative team was asked to work on an important brief.

The belief at Ulka was that to be competitive externally we needed to be collaborative internally. There have been numerous occasions when briefs from one office were worked on by creative teams in another city or a baseline from one team was adopted by other teams working on the campaign.

One of our most successful campaigns was for Hero Pleasure scooters, where the strategic insight was developed by the Delhi account planning team, the creative magnifier 'Why should boys have all the fun' came from the Bangalore office and the final script with Priyanka Chopra as Manjeet (the silly village girl!) was crafted by the Delhi creative team.

Another example is the Tata Motors campaign for the Indigo launch, where the print ad was created by the Delhi creative team based on a brief from Mumbai.

INTERDEPENDENCE VS INDEPENDENCE

At Ulka, the leadership shared very similar backgrounds—each member held an MBA from one of the IIMs and all had extensive experience in advertising and marketing, with many having worked together before joining Ulka. Despite these similarities, each leader possessed a unique personality and leadership style. However, this group successfully stayed together and operated as a great team for over 25 years. The key to this cohesion lay in the genius of Anil Kapoor, who recognized the different personalities and assigned roles that best suited each individual. He united the team with a common purpose and shared values, fostering complete transparency within the senior team. The matrix structure also helped match the strengths and weaknesses of individual members.

This trust and interdependence extended to the levels below. The second and third lines in the organization were woven together with the same values and common purpose. Anil acted as a coach and mentor to each one of us and, over the years, helped to smoothen out the rough edges in relationships in a firm but fair manner. Every individual was discussed openly in a forum and no grudges were held after the meeting concluded.

The matrix structure supported interdependence and decisions were made through a consensus-building process, albeit slow and tedious at times, ensuring buy-in from all constituents. The larger good always served as the touchstone for decision-making. There were innumerable instances of a business head sacrificing or not pursuing a business if it adversely affected another business unit.

An illustrative example involved Ulka Delhi winning the account of the only large Indian fast-moving consumer goods (FMCG) company in the city—an achievement considering other FMCG accounts were globally aligned and hence closed to us. After a couple of years of handling various brands, the client decided to reorganize the brand portfolio among the aligned agencies and assigned Ulka the dental range of products. Simultaneously, Ulka Calcutta, which had been struggling to survive due to the corporate exodus from the city, secured entry into a business with a competing dental range. As per industry ethics, we could not have handled both businesses without getting approval from both clients. In this case, the Delhi client, a significant advertiser, declined the agency's request to handle the competing brand and was unwilling to allot us a non-competing category. In the larger interest, the Delhi office gave up its client so that the Calcutta office could retain its business. Over the years, Delhi went on to acquire other FMCG businesses but unfortunately could not regain the clients it gave up. However, I have never regretted giving up the Delhi client for the Calcutta office.

Savita Mathai joined the agency as a management trainee in the Star One programme and is currently the group's chief talent officer at FCB India and IPG Mediabrands. Savita recalls:

In the late 1980s, a management training (MT) programme was not uncommon. In fact, all large, self-respecting companies engaged in campus recruitment because it was a good source of talent acquisition. What set Ulka apart was that its MT programme was not only a talent acquisition strategy but also a culture-building strategy. For an advertising agency to visit some of the most prestigious B-schools in the country and compete with all the FMCG giants (during the glorious era of marketing when marketing jobs were the most coveted) required more than gumption. It demanded a long-term plan, unwavering commitment and deep passion.

And that is what the Star One programme was all about. It was a mission led by Anil and his leadership team to bring in quality talent and nurture them into leaders. These were individuals who embraced the values and belief system of the company early on, becoming its evangelists—to propagating it, one batch at a time. 'An army of mercenaries never won a war,' Anil would say. 'We need an army of believers.' Star One was his way of building an army of believers. Year after year, regardless of economic booms or busts, a new batch of trainees would be inducted. Eventually, most people managing key accounts and functions in the agency were individuals who had grown within the company, the Star One way.

I happened to be part of one of the earliest Star One batches. Because Star One held such significance for Anil, the entire process was managed solely by the top management. It was a comprehensive three-month programme, akin to leaving management school to join advertising school and getting paid for it. The programme was designed to not only impart on-the-job skills but also to provide invaluable life lessons, help forge lifelong friendships and inculcate a love for the business of advertising.

In the welcome session, Anil spoke of many things—not principles of marketing, advertising strategy or any of that. There was one thing he said and it stuck with me forever: 'To be a good professional, you first need to be a good human being.'

That one session with him taught us Anil's simple life truths:

- *If you truly loved something, you could not help but excel at it.*
- *If you genuinely believed in something, success was bound to be yours.*
- *Most importantly, life was finally all about relationships. If you invested in partnerships, your mission would be accomplished.*

Seeing him in action for 25 years after that, one realized that this was the philosophy he lived and breathed. And built an institution on passion, the courage of conviction and undying partnerships.

It all went down in the agency's culture book as 'Attitude trumps Aptitude'.

SIX

ADVERTISING IS A SENIOR PERSON'S BUSINESS

'Experience is that marvellous thing that enables you to recognize a mistake when you make it again.'

—Franklin P. Jones

Anil Kapoor usually said, 'Advertising is a senior person's business where the best ideas come from youngsters.' It does seem to be a bit of a contradiction for a business where the average age is in the twenties. However, when one looks at the history of client–agency relationships that have resulted in great brand-building campaigns, a common factor emerges—the close partnership at senior levels between the agency and the client. This is not restricted to advertising but holds true for any consultancy business where the service organization is a strategic partner to the client company.

While advertising plays a pivotal role in creating brand value, it cannot work in isolation; it needs to operate in cohesion with the other elements of the marketing mix. Therefore, advertising's role in creating brand value is only possible if it is in sync with the overall marketing strategy. In other words, the agency must be aware of and/or involved in the client's product, price and distribution strategies. For this to happen, the agency must have the trust and respect of the senior-most levels at the client's end.

In almost every case where successful brand-building activity has resulted in creating brand value for a company, there has been a close relationship between the senior levels at the agency and similar levels at the client end. Advertising history is filled with stories and anecdotes of such relationships. Claude Hopkins, Fairfax Cone, David Ogilvy and Bill Bernbach were close partners to their client CEOs. In the Indian context too, Subhas Ghosal, Subroto Sengupta, Mani Iyer, Bal Mundkur and Alyque Padamsee were all partners with senior clients.

In each of these cases, a senior person at the agency, either the managing director (MD), CEO or national creative director (NCD), had an active involvement in the business. The agency's point of view extended beyond the brief given by the marketing department, incorporating an added business perspective gained through interactions with the senior-most levels in the client organization.

Often, briefs to the agency lack clarity on what advertising is expected to deliver and, in many cases, are not in sync with the overall marketing imperatives facing the company. They are created at a level in the marketing department that does not have a full picture of the strategic issues facing the company. In other cases, it's a second-guessing exercise of what the brand manager thinks their bosses want. Consequently, campaigns are often rejected at the final approval stage because, while they may have passed the test of creativity, they are not aligned with the perspective of the senior levels in the client organization. This underscores the critical role of senior agency personnel being involved and connected with senior levels at the client organization in a productive relationship.

An agency is fortunate if it encounters a brand manager with the perspective and courage to put forward a new, different and unconventional idea. However, most often, brand managers are empowered with the authority to say no rather than yes to something that goes beyond the brief. This leads to a surplus of ideas within agencies, many of which never progress beyond the first stage, not to mention those killed by overzealous suits within the agency itself!

Here again, a senior team member at the agency needs to be involved to recognize good ideas that may be unconventional and chaperone such ideas through the maze at both the agency's and the client's end. Good ideas need protection and nurturing, akin to precious stones. In the early stages, good ideas are often rough, raw and unpolished, requiring patience and crafting to bring out their brilliance.

Breakthrough ideas almost always come with attached risks. There is no precedent to judge whether they will work or not, necessitating the judgement of a senior agency person to provide credibility and reassurance that the idea has a reasonable chance of delivering results. At the client's end, it takes courage and trust in the agency, along with assurance from someone senior, that the risk is worth taking.

At Ulka, every member of the board had developed a professional relationship with the senior-most levels of all major clients. Therefore, for clients like Tata Motors, Zee, Amul, LML, Usha, Hero Honda and Tropicana, the agency's recommendations impacted strategic marketing decisions related to product, pricing and distribution and not just advertising. Anil had personal relationships with every major client MD/chairman and they would reach out to him for issues beyond advertising.

Ambi Parameswaran, the CEO of FCB Ulka, Mumbai, and founder of brandbuilding.com, a coach and an author, recollects a memorable incident.

The Tata Motors boardroom on the first floor of Bombay House boasted a very long table. As one of India's biggest companies, Tata Motors had a rather formidable board and the grandeur of the boardroom, table and gizmos reflected the size and stature of the company. While the long table could easily accommodate over 16 people, there was also additional provision for another 15 individuals to be seated in an outer ring. Tata Motors was an important account for the FCB Ulka group, which meant that Anil Kapoor and I were closely involved in all aspects of the business. Most of our meetings with the client team used to start around 5 p.m. and stretch way into the night. This is the story of one such meeting.

Anil and I walked into Bombay House with a sizeable agency team consisting of more than seven people. There were many issues to be discussed and presentations to be made. As we walked into the boardroom, Mr Krishnan, the Head of Commercial of Tata Motors Passenger Business Unit, was already seated, deep in conversation with Nitin Seth and a product manager. The moment we walked in, Krishnan was effusive in his welcome. 'Mr Kapoor, so good to see you after a while!' Mr Kapoor had to gently remind him that we had been in the same room just 10 days earlier for another discussion. Nevertheless, he was very appreciative of the fact that the MD of the agency group paid so much personal attention to the fortunes of the brands of Tata Motors.

Mr Rajiv Dube joined us a few minutes later and observing the number of people in the room said, 'You guys outnumber us two to one!' Anil laughed and quipped that the casting vote was always with the client.

I explained that we had done a deep dive into the new brand plans and had a presentation to share with the client, requesting two hours of their time. I recall Mr Dube saying, 'Well, we are at your command!'

We used to have a way of sitting at the table. The projector was in the middle and the large screen was at one end. The presenter usually stood at the screen end. I used to sit close to that end, next to Anil, who could make eye contact with Mr Dube and Mr Krishnan. Next to Anil would be the seat for the client services director, followed by the creative director, the planning head, the account director, the account planning supervisor and so on. It was almost the hierarchy of the agency on display.

I requested Ruta, who had taken charge as head of planning of the account, to make the presentation.

As she got up to present, Mr Dube could not resist and said, 'Wow, you are going to present. I remember you sitting at that end of the table. Now you have moved to this end. Mr Kapoor, you should explain this logic to us.'

Anil, at this point, delivered his million-dollar comment, 'Sir, we, as an agency, believe that advertising is a senior person's business, but the best ideas come from the youngsters.'

'What do you mean by that, sir?' asked Mr Krishnan.

'Well, Mr Krishan, you know that Ambi and I are here for all critical meetings. We don't leave it to the youngsters to handle critical accounts, especially when senior leaders on the client side are taking time out to meet the agency. But the best ideas do not come from us. They come from youngsters like Ruta. So we select them carefully and ensure that they move up rapidly. Ruta was at that end, sitting as a young account executive, carrying artwork to the meeting. Now she is heading account planning, standing up to present to you. So advertising

is a senior person's business, but ideas and energy come from the youngsters,' Anil explained.

This cultural attribute created a strong bond at every level in the organization. The most junior person was encouraged to contribute their ideas, and senior team members fostered an environment where youngsters could express their views without fear of being cut down to size. In creative teams, juniors were asked to present their own ideas and if an idea was shortlisted, the team leaders were expected to prepare the junior to present the idea at client meetings.

SEVEN

NEVER BUY PEOPLE

'The real measure of your wealth is how much you'd be worth if you lost all your money.'

—Benjamin Jowett

The myth of universal selfishness has a compelling force in most modern organizations. If you want your employees to work harder, the common approach is to tie their salaries to performance. Similarly, to encourage senior management to maximize returns for the shareholders, companies often resort to incentivizing them with stock options or profit-sharing schemes.

During the post-liberalization period, rapid economic growth outpaced the supply of talent, leading to a significant reduction in the average tenure of marketing professionals—from years to mere months. The advertising industry, in particular, also witnessed an era of double-digit growth accompanied by a high turnover of personnel. The driving force behind this turnover was the allure of financial gain, as money proved to be a strong catalyst for job changes. Many agencies began to adopt a strategy of implementing two or more cycles of salary increments each year, departing from the traditional annual increment model in order to feed this constant hunger for growth (interpreted as more money). While this phenomenon was somewhat understandable in the early years of economic liberalization, given the context of a country and an industry that had endured decades of low salaries and substantial disparities compared to international pay scales, the gap has since considerably narrowed.

At Ulka, we stuck to some basic principles when it came to rewarding and motivating our people. The result was a significantly lower turnover of personnel compared to the industry average—indicating that something must have worked.

THE FIRST PRINCIPLE

The temptation to quickly acquire talent, whatever the cost, when there are gaps to fill due to an exit or securing a large new business is immense. However, like many quick fixes, this is often a short-term solution that unravels very soon. Individuals who join for monetary reasons also tend to leave, sooner rather than later, for better financial offers elsewhere. In our recruitment process at Ulka, we made a deliberate effort to understand why a person was seeking a change, their reasons for moving, expectations from a new job and whether we could offer the kind of motivating environment and work they were looking for.

On numerous occasions, I chose not to proceed with candidates who appeared opportunistic, hoping to extract an unreasonable salary or a higher designation beyond industry norms or our organizational structure. I was particularly cautious about individuals who had changed jobs frequently to advance beyond what their capabilities or experience warranted.

I often advised those who left us for seemingly irresistible offers in terms of money or designations to be mindful of the golden handcuffs. Receiving a salary or designation significantly beyond one's level is always suspicious and more often leads to individuals being trapped in a job they dislike but can't leave because equivalent job opportunities are scarce in the industry.

THE SECOND PRINCIPLE

Never short-change your existing team by bringing in someone with a similar profile or experience as your current employees and then paying the newcomer more or assigning them a higher designation. At our agency, we prioritized transparency in our remuneration structure and designations, refusing to compromise to accommodate a new hire. While salaries and designations underwent periodic reviews aligned with industry norms, these adjustments were never impulsive reactions. Given our system of annual increments, individuals joining between increment cycles either committed to receiving the increment with the rest of the organization or, if offered a higher package upon joining, understood they would not be entitled to any in the immediately following increment cycle. The approach was grounded in the belief that employees cannot be expected to stay if they feel it's always better to be rehired or the only time to secure a better deal is during the initial hiring phase.

THE THIRD PRINCIPLE

We encouraged our team members to return to us because we felt it was a reinforcement of our organizational culture. Those coming back were familiar with what they were returning to and, hopefully, had a greater appreciation for the culture and environment, having missed it when they were away. In several instances, ex-employees expressed a desire to rejoin within months of leaving, and in almost all cases, they had departed for a significantly higher salary and designation.

However, in each one of these cases we welcomed them back under the condition that they return on the same salary and designation they would have held had they stayed on in the agency. If at all we reconsidered their package, it was always at the time of annual increments, aligning with the adjustments for others at the same level.

THE FOURTH PRINCIPLE

At Ulka, rewards were delivered over time and manifested in various forms beyond monetary compensation. There was a constant effort to motivate high performers by offering them more challenging assignments and greater independence. Opportunities such as attending senior client meetings, participating in strategy discussions and presenting campaigns to clients were given, offering invaluable learning experiences. In all departments, young talents were encouraged to present their ideas to senior management, fostering confidence in making presentations to clients. This practice also allowed senior leaders to identify promising individuals at an early stage. Unlike many agencies where only senior creatives worked on major campaigns or film ideas, at Ulka, this opportunity was extended at a relatively early age.

The company also followed a unique approach of keeping senior positions vacant to pave the way for bright talents to step in, instead of hindering their growth by recruiting externally.

Sanjeev Bhargava joined Ulka Delhi in 1993 after earning an MBA from the Faculty of Management Studies, University of Delhi, one of the premier business schools, accumulating six years of experience in Lintas and HTA. Early on at Ulka it was felt that he was someone who had the makings of a top-class advertising professional. However, within a year, Sanjeev received a very attractive offer from another agency, with a substantial salary hike and a higher designation. Sanjeev was happy at Ulka but was obviously attracted to the terms he was being offered. I talked him into staying back on the assurance that the opportunities he would get at Ulka over the years would outweigh the immediate gain he was seeking.

To his credit, Sanjeev stayed back without any commitment to salary or designation, and sure enough, the opportunity came within the next six months. He stayed on with the agency for 17 years, rising to become the chief operating officer of the Delhi office and a member of the executive council. Later in his career, he led the JWT Delhi office and served as the brand director at *The Times of India*. He is currently a consultant, investor and restaurant owner.

Reflecting on this experience and tenure at Ulka, Sanjeev shares:

I joined Ulka in 1993 and immediately fell in love with the organization. Looking back, it was a simple combination of:

1. *No personal agendas*
2. *An environment of interpersonal appreciation and encouragement*
3. *Unwavering confidence in the organizational ability to meet client expectations*

Most of this stemmed from the Ulka cultural philosophy, not only articulated but practised on a daily basis. I was lucky to catch the industry's attention as soon as I joined, receiving offers almost weekly from competing organizations. One offer was particularly juicy and tempted me, but by then a few months had passed and I was hooked on to the Ulka culture and the people I worked with, especially Arvind Wable and Nitish Mukherjee, both of whom took pains to help me grow as an advertising professional.

I did not have the heart to take up the competing offer, which not only tripled my CTC but also propelled me to senior management in a fairly reputed organization. As per the Ulka culture, no immediate rewards or enticements were offered to me by the organization to stay on. But Arvind did promise that I would not regret it.

Sure enough, in about six months, I was asked to pack my bags and go to Ulka Calcutta as the branch manager. I was 32 with barely eight years under my belt.

The branch was collapsing, with most clients on the verge of leaving. Anil Kapoor punted on me. 'Try your best. If it doesn't work, you will be back to your job in Delhi. No questions asked.'

When you have the permission to fail and the determination to succeed, magic happens. The first challenge was the inexperience of the staff and their despondency about the future. Leading by example, leading from the front and showing that success was possible was the only way out. A small victory, the acquisition of a minuscule new business of a coconut oil brand, galvanized the entire team. That was the first new business acquisition in the Calcutta office in eight years! They all wanted to be part of a new success story. They not only wanted to participate and contribute but, most importantly, learn.

In the spirit of the Ulka culture, which I had imbibed by then, I started nurturing the team—taking evening classes on advertising strategy, creativity and operations. It was a small team, but in a span of a few months, it was a committed team raring to go.

As a result, we started winning business. We were a breath of fresh air in the city, bringing in learnings from my experiences at Unilever, Nestle and Pepsi to bear on local clients. Whether I needed strategic planning support for a pitch or a film executive for a film we were making in-house for an important client, help was always at hand. Shashi Sinha gave me a free hand but was always there if I wanted his advice.

We became the fastest growing advertising agency in the city and maintained a relentless pace for the three years that I was there. We turned profitable and were celebrated by the city as well as the rest of the organization.

From a decaying entity to a vibrant growing office, the transformation over my three-year stint was a joyful and triumphant journey, which I consider the best phase of my advertising career.

More successes were in store for me in the future, but nothing compared to the love and joy that was created as a by-product of our success during my stint in Calcutta.

To me, this was yet another emphatic demonstration of what the Ulkaway could do.

THE PARTNERSHIP PROGRAMME

Ulka was among the first agencies in the country to introduce an annual partnership programme. Consciously, it was not labelled as an incentive or performance programme. The Partnership Programme (PP) at Ulka reflected the agency's values of teamwork and consistent performance. Unlike many incentive programmes, the final reward was not determined by an individual or committee but was completely transparent. A significant portion of the reward was based on company performance, followed by team performance and finally, qualitative factors.

Another unique aspect of the PP was the proportion it constituted within the annual package. At the senior most levels, it ranged from 30 per cent to 40 per cent of the total remuneration package. This had two implications: first, everyone worked for the greater good rather than their individual domains, and second, it showcased an entrepreneurial spirit where the team shared in the company's progress and profits instead of insulating themselves from the fortunes of the company by having high fixed salary components immune to the company's performance.

The PP was initiated at the management board level and gradually trickled down to the level of the account executive or equivalent across all functions. The programme delivered consistently year after year, strengthening the spirit of teamwork, consistent performance and transparency within the agency.

The Ulka values were reflected in every aspect of the agency's operations, most notably in the teams cultivated over two decades. The values of loyalty and partnership, along with fairness and transparency in the reward system, made it a preferred workplace. Even those who left departed with goodwill for the time spent at Ulka.

EIGHT

PRIMA DONNAS

'By coddling the prima donna, you are abdicating your responsibility for leadership.'

—Anonymous

Advertising has always been a business with attitude, attracting edgy, creative and maverick individuals. Some of the most iconic brand-building campaigns were executed by people with colourful lives and unique habits, as agencies traditionally have always embraced and honoured creative genius—and rightly so. Many legendary names in advertising emerged from the creative realm.

Anecdotal evidence, whether true or embellished, has fuelled the mystique surrounding the glamorous side of advertising, akin to the atmosphere portrayed in *Mad Men*. Stories of copywriters taking briefs at the Olympia bar in Calcutta after 11.30 a.m., office affairs, the wild parties including those that ended in fisticuffs followed by reconciliations the next day, the week-long depressive boozing binges after losing an account or a pitch have added to the allure of the advertising business. Bohemian dress codes, ponytails and large handlebars were all part of the charm.

The true geniuses in advertising were highly gifted, passionate individuals driven by their personal vision. They created enduring agency brands, leaving a rich legacy that continues to be celebrated across generations.

Unfortunately, over the years, many of the hotshots were those propelled into the industry limelight by one or two award-winning campaigns, contributing to a culture where agencies focused solely on awards. This approach led to the emergence of prima donnas, whose dominance and individualistic approach often resulted in low team spirit, a highly competitive agency environment, bruised egos and a high turnover of talent.

This is in no way an attempt to diminish the great value and impact of the advertising industry and brands derived from the constant presence of a few great creative personalities. Their talent and passion have driven creative standards to a new high and significantly influenced the fortunes of undifferentiated brands. However, their creative dominance occasionally overwhelmed weak-kneed marketing managers into accepting scripts or ideas they might not approve of if presented by a less celebrated creative director.

What we need in the industry today are leaders who understand that advertising is about delivering results and building sustainable brand equity for clients rather than just pursuing award-winning campaigns. Brilliant minds, whether in creative, strategy or media, need to understand the value of building great brands.

Ulka's focus on strategy and creating effective advertising that worked for the brand sometimes created a perception that the agency did not value or encourage good creatives. Emphasis on teamwork kept away those who were too individualistic to conform to a team structure, making it challenging to attract good creative talent who understood the value of teamwork and the contribution of good strategy. However, those who joined stayed with the agency, contributing to brand-building campaigns for Santoor, Sundrop, Whirlpool, Naukri, Indica, Tropicana, Docomo, Pleasure Scooters, etc.

While creative leadership at Ulka may not have garnered as much media attention as their award-winning counterparts, each member earned the respect of clients for creating memorable campaigns such as, 'More car per car',[8] 'Hari Sadu',[9] 'Meri twacha se meri umra ka pata hi nahin chalta',[10] 'Mummy ka magic chalega kya',[11] 'Healthy oil for healthy people'[12] and 'Why should boys have all the fun'.[13]

Ulka had a distinct culture epitomized by the absence of prima donnas; it was always a team of talented individuals with shared values and a common purpose. This not only resulted in stability within the senior team across functions—be it management or servicing, strategy, creative or media—but also fostered strong and stable client relationships. There was hardly an instance of a client leaving the agency or calling for a review because one individual left the agency or moved off the account. At Ulka, we were also wary of working with external talent that behaved like prima donnas.

---

[8] Tata Indica V2 (2005); More car per car, YouTube, https://www.youtube.com/watch?v=oEF5sptyM6o.

[9] Naukri.com Hari Sadu, YouTube, https://www.youtube.com/watch?v=q6uYXDT9PyA.

[10] Santoor Bookshop (1989–93), YouTube, https://www.youtube.com/watch?v=y2jHheBM0pk.

[11] Whirlpool Whitemagic—Mummy Ka Magic, YouTube, https://www.youtube.com/watch?v=rTWwBc1Soyg.

[12] Sundrop—Mom & Son (Cartwheel), YouTube, https://www.youtube.com/watch?v=dH71FBR6Q_I.

[13] Hero Honda Pleasure (2006), YouTube, https://www.youtube.com/watch?v=HI5MmRYqfWA.

Ambi Parmeswaran recounts one such case.

'Hey Ambi, do something for me,' was a plea from a leading ad filmmaker. He had created numerous ads for FCB Ulka in the past, working across Mumbai, Delhi and Bangalore clients. The teams loved him and he enjoyed working with us. However, something had happened.

'Look, VK [name changed], there is a problem and you know why you have not been getting any new films from us for the last two years. We love you, man. But there is an issue, and you know it,' I replied, adding, 'You are a sought-after filmmaker and you get many films. Forget we exist and get on with your life, man. Life is too short to keep worrying about past sins.'

'It is not as if I don't get films, Ambi. I do get enough work. But your agency is different. Do you know that last month my accountant got a call from your Delhi office saying that they were sending us something to the tune of ₹15 lakh owed to us for over three years because the client had not paid? Now that the client has paid, your guys called to pay us. No agency does this. They hope that we have forgotten the payment that is due to us. And I like you guys. Tell me what I can do, Ambi!' was his response.

'VK, you need to meet AK to sort this out. I can't solve the problem, neither can the film manager. You got to meet AK and you need to be ready to take some heavy-duty brickbats for what you did,' I said.

'Hey, AK is refusing to take my call. You set up the meeting and I will show up like a little puppy,' VK demurred.

'VK, it is not just that you have to listen to AK; you need to internalize what he has to say. Are you ready for that? It will be a bitter medicine, as you may have gathered.'

'Yes, I will swallow the medicine. Just set up the meeting,' VK murmured.

We shook hands and I promised to get back to him in a day or two. It took some persuasion to get AK to give time to VK. He warned me that VK might refuse to work with us in the future after the session. I told him, 'So be it. He wanted it. Let him have it!'

AK's assistant was requested to slot a session for VK in the coming week. I acted as the go-between to ensure that VK arrived on time; more often than not, he was a perpetual late-lateef, a habitual latecomer. However, he was there early, had a cup of coffee with me to boost his morale and I ushered him into AK's cabin, beating a hasty retreat.

I was not in the room but I can imagine what would have transpired. Here is my version of it.

'VK, I heard you wanted to meet me. Tell me why you were so keen on meeting me.'

'AK, you are my favourite person to work for. I have done so many ads for your agency and half my showreel is your ads. But I have not received any ads from your agency for the last two years and I wanted to know why.'

'You know why. Tell me, why do you think we are not giving you any films?'

'I realize that I made a mistake. At the shoot in Australia, I had no business to threaten your team...' He was not allowed to finish before AK jumped in.

'VK, you are a dimwit. We have stood behind you through thick and thin. Remember when AM wanted to change the director for the film we were making for the new car; we stood like a rock behind you and you did this to us.' AK did not let go. 'Yes, there was an operational issue and you had to incur some extra cost, but you had no business to threaten to call off the shoot and put on a big-shot act. We don't tolerate prima donnas in our agency, as you would have realized by now!'

'No prima donnas?'

'Yes, VK, you may be a big star and you may get mobbed in airports, but when you work with us, you have to leave your ego at the entrance gate and behave as a member of the team. We don't allow anyone to play the big-shot. I may be the big boss to all my colleagues, but they are welcome to disagree with all that I say. Often, I don't have the last word. So when we don't tolerate prima donnas internally, do you think we will tolerate the prima donna act from a film-maker? No way,' AK thundered.

'AK, I am sorry for what I did. I promise I will behave myself. I realized that the issue was not about money but about my behaviour. I should have behaved better. I will not repeat this, but please give me another chance,' VK pleaded softly.

'Okay,' said AK, 'Now that is behind us. Here is an interesting film idea I wanted to bounce off you...'

Two hours later, VK popped into my cabin to say thank you. I could not resist asking, 'VK, did you learn your lesson?'

'Yes. No prima donnas.'

NINE

NO ZERO NO HERO OVERNIGHT

'Success is a journey, not a destination.'

—Ben Sweetland

The saying 'You are as good as your last campaign' is something one often hears in the agency circuit, prevalent not only among clients who switch agencies on a regular basis but also within the agencies themselves.

Traditionally, advertising has been an industry where talent receives early recognition, leading to quick promotions, fancier designations and, of course, increased compensation. The high achievers in agency systems often ascend rapidly and, just as swiftly, exit once they realize their value.

In this environment, the policy of 'No Zero No Hero Overnight (NZNHO)' was clearly contrary to accepted norms, yet that is exactly what Ulka upheld as one of its core values for over 20 years. The agency faced accusations at times of encouraging mediocrity over meritocracy, with debates on batch processing versus individual merit recognition surfacing at the time of annual increments. Despite facing criticisms, the effectiveness of the Ulka system was evident in the quality of individuals the agency has always had and, more importantly, retained for over two decades. In industry circles, it was widely acknowledged that luring talented professionals away from Ulka was very difficult.

The fundamentals of NZNHO were based on two critical factors—transparency and fairness. Every individual joining the agency was aware of how the system operated, the philosophy behind it and its equitable application to everyone, irrespective of their levels or departments.

Meritocracy is an essential part of any successful organization, particularly in an industry like advertising where the core competency lies in the quality of talent. The fundamental question is—how is merit defined and judged? At Ulka, it was defined as consistent performance, not based solely on the last piece of work done. Also, when viewed in the context of other Ulka values such as attitude versus aptitude and a focus on teams over individuals, the NZNHO policy became an intrinsic part of the overall culture.

Consequently, the growth path for most individuals in the first five years of their career at Ulka was relatively similar and predictable. The logic behind this approach was to provide equal opportunities before categorizing individuals as high performers, medium performers or underperformers.

Let's take the scenario of a young creative or servicing professional joining a large mainline agency with multiple accounts, varying in size from large to small, encompassing both global MNCs and Indian corporates. Each of these clients will exhibit different spending levels, varied relationships with the agency and diverse cultures. Within the agency itself, there will be different subcultures, depending on the GM, vice president or creative director with whom one gets to work. It is often the luck of the draw or availability of specific slots that determines where young entrants begin their career.

For instance, working with a client who values agency inputs, believes in brand building and allocates significant funds to multimedia campaigns is the agency's dream client. This gives the young entrant a flying start and great exposure across functions in the agency.

On the other hand, if they get assigned to an equally large client, perhaps a public sector unit, with substantial budgets, primarily releasing print ads and an occasional film every few years, the dynamics change. When the main contact at the client's end is the publicity manager, it presents a completely different world. Alternatively, the client might be aligned with global brands, being a significant spender, but with most strategy and positioning determined at a global level. In this case, the local agency is expected to adapt or adopt the international creative work, involving substantial coordination with the global or regional office and adherence to a strictly laid-down process of creative development, report submission, billing, collections, etc.

Consider the worst-case scenario where a young executive or copywriter is assigned to the most challenging or disliked account in the agency (every agency has its share), an account that is extremely demanding but currently has limited spending in the hope that one day it will turn into a significant business for the agency.

Hence, the opportunities and challenges in each case are markedly different. Therefore, when evaluating performances, especially at the operating levels (1–5-year experience), one must consider qualitative factors such as understanding the client's business, anticipating client needs, ability to manage difficult situations, ability to handle client relationships and adhering to procedures. These factors are best measured over time.

In numerous cases, individuals who struggled on one account found success when moved to another. Clients often voice complaints about someone on the agency team. While the feedback is taken seriously, the initial reaction is not to remove the person from the account. Instead, a senior figure steps in to understand where the relationship is faltering. Many times, the problem lies with the client and, in such cases, the issue is taken up to the senior level. Instances exist when client feedback led to an apology and, in some cases, changes on the client's end.

One notable instance occurred when Ulka secured a new client with a lottery licence; the company was a large family conglomerate involved in varied businesses. The lottery business was established as a separate entity with one of the sons of the family as the managing director. We won the business through a competitive pitch based on our strategy. The relationship began positively, with the agency's strategy being approved by the client and the presentation of some great campaigns to them. Eventually, one campaign received approval from the young managing director. The next stage involved the MD getting the buy-in for the campaign from the family. This became an endless exercise of iterations with comments and views from individual family members being accommodated. Unfortunately, the original campaign started losing its essence and we were running out of time as the launch date approached. In a meeting intended for final approval, the young MD requested more changes. The agency team leader attempted to reason with the MD, requesting not to make the changes in the interest of creative rendition of the campaign as well as the shortage of time. The MD threw a fit, shouting and abusing. I was present at the meeting, and as soon as the MD finished his rant, I instructed the team to get up and leave. I informed the MD that we would give up the business unless he apologized to the agency team leader. To his credit, the young MD did apologize and we got the campaign approved without any further changes.

As we exited the meeting, the agency team leader turned to me and said, 'Arvind, thank you for standing up for me. It's my birthday today and this is the best gift I could have got.'

Recognizing team effort over individual performance is another crucial aspect. Success in the agency context often stems from the collective contributions of various team members. This includes the account team that takes the brief, the account planning person who crafts the proposition, the young creative who generates the idea, the CD who guides the process and transforms it into a campaign and the media person who sells the innovative media idea to the client and flawlessly executes it through the chosen channel or publication.

Once again, making heroes or zeros without due consideration of the team's input would be unfair. Individual contributions to the team need to be evaluated over time. The concern expressed often is that better performers get frustrated due to what can be perceived as a batch processing system. This is even more evident in today's environment when everybody, especially youngsters, wants to move up fast—both monetarily and professionally.

While a system of rewards for good or outstanding performance is essential, it does not have to be limited to promotions and increments only. At Ulka, the reward system took many forms, including greater responsibilities, more freedom in terms of lesser supervision, independent client meetings, participation in pitches and making client presentations. This enabled the quick starters to gain recognition and grow while providing opportunities for others to catch up and realize their full potential. It's quite like a sprinter versus a long-distance runner—both can be as valuable to the company if their individual traits are given equal opportunity.

It was only after the first five years that the merit-based system became more prominent. Here again, efforts were made to help individuals succeed, transferring those not working well in one account or group to another with the hope that things will work out for the better. The agency had an unwritten rule that no senior would make a scapegoat of a junior when things went wrong. It was okay to reprimand or pull up people, but it was the senior's responsibility to fix things and bear the brunt of the problem upfront. Further, all appraisals and evaluations were conducted by the person's supervisor in the presence of the supervisor's superior to ensure impartiality. If the person still did not improve, only then would the agency suggest that they seek another job.

The NZNHO approach was difficult to implement and there were times when good people left for supposedly greener pastures. However, those who stayed added immense value to the agency over the years. The most satisfying thing was when many who left returned, some within a few months and others after several years, because they appreciated the transparency and fairness of the Ulka system. In fact, the average tenure of the senior team at the agency exceeded 10 years, with many returning after working a couple of years in other agencies, more appreciative and committed to the Ulkaway.

Niteen Bhagwat was vice chairman of FCB Interface and is now the director of Karira Consulting. He recalls:

Very early in our journey with Anil, we experienced the term 'prime mover'. We knew the meaning but learned first-hand what it really meant. For most of us who had worked in other organizations before Ulka, leading a project meant that you took the decisions, you were the boss and you carried the responsibility.

It was late evening (as it always was) when I presented on a project and announced the decisions I had taken. As was his habit, Anil hit the pause button and asked the others for their opinions. Several hours of debate later, we were no closer to a solution. Exhausted, I asked, 'So what is the point of having a prime mover?' Anil, I think, was waiting for the question. He launched into a little story and concluded that a 'prime mover' on a project is only the first among equals. There must be consensus on every major decision and no one has absolute authority on any decision. In other words, there are no prima donnas or bosses in the team. Listen to the others, swallow your pride and remember that every decision must be embraced by everyone on the team.

One day, I was in my room discussing a campaign when I heard a knock, and a young lad peeped in. He was among the brightest of our management trainees, liked by the teams, loved by the client and always delivered. He clearly looked distraught and was working up an anger. I closed the meeting and beckoned him in. No sooner did he sit down than the dam burst, and the upsets started pouring out. He had just received his increment letter and was horrified to discover that his increment was the same as everyone's in his batch. He pointed out that even those who clearly were not doing well had got the same increment.

I smiled and vividly remembered a similar conversation

that I had had with Anil. I said, 'Beta, remember, in a team, there are "No Heroes and No Zeros". You should never pass judgement on performances over just a year. All of us know you are good at your work, but you also have a very supportive and responsible client, and you also have a boss who really knows what to do. The choice of the boss or client is not in your control, so you must realize that some of the great work that you are doing is because of the circumstances. God forbid if you had a really difficult client and a boss who could not manage the client—would it have been fair to penalize you for a subpar performance?' Grudgingly, he accepted the reason.

A decade later, our trainee, who had since left the agency to get into marketing, came to visit. He had done very well for himself, and the visit was to thank all of us at the agency for the culture code that was imprinted in his mind. For the next hour, he regaled us on how he told his juniors the meaning of family, of non-evaluative conversations and, most importantly, that at Ulka there were no prima donnas, and no individual was a hero or a zero.

I smiled, understanding what Anil must have felt when he took the first culture 'paathshala' on team building and prima donnas.

TEN

NO TURF WARS

'I have yet to find the man, however exalted his station, who did not do better work and put forth greater effort under a spirit of approval than under a spirit of criticism.'

—Charles Schwab

Once on a bus, you have as much right to be on it as every other person already on it. On the Ulka bus, you would get on only if you had the right aptitude and the right attitude. So once you are on it, you are okay.

The idea of a non-evaluative relationship is often misunderstood to mean no evaluation. It is confused with the lack of feedback, absence of appraisals or lack of supervision. This is far from the truth. In a non-evaluative culture, there is constant evaluation and feedback except the evaluation is of the issue and not the person. What is discussed is how you handled the issue and not who you are.

It takes a lot of effort and heartburn to create a non-evaluative culture within a team because egos are fragile and get bruised and sometimes broken easily. Each person comes on to the team with a baggage of past experiences and sensitivities. Each individual comes with a distinct personality. The key to building a non-evaluative culture within the group is by being conscious of the differences and accepting them and, more importantly, assimilating them into the team culture.

A secure environment wherein one does not have to prove one's worth every day is critical to non-evaluative relationships. You have to believe that if you are in the team, you are worth it and are there to add value to the output of the team. So there are no heroes or zeros overnight. The focus is to learn and grow. Make small mistakes and learn big. A long rope is given, not to hang oneself but to guide one back to the ship even if someone goes astray.

At Ulka, the non-evaluative culture started at the senior most levels of the company—the management board (MB) level. The MB was made up of six members: the MD, four CEOs and the CFO. Each CEO looked after a specific business area. There were a lot of commonalities in the backgrounds of the board members. In spite of all the similarities, each one had a very different personality and operating style as a manager.

The challenge was to have this group at the top to have a non-evaluative relationship. To do this, Anil had laid down some ground rules:

1. All decisions will be made by consensus.
2. One for all, all for one—it is never any one person's problem, challenge or opportunity.
3. A matrix structure wherein each person was dependent on others to meet individual business objectives.
4. All issues, good and bad, were discussed by the group. No one was to shove anything under the carpet—ever.
5. A partnership programme (year-end performance bonus) based predominantly on the company's achievement rather than individual achievements.

6. A common set of values that were to be practised or propagated within the organization by each board member.
7. Disagreements and discussions were encouraged.
8. No one was to carry grudges or hurt outside the board meetings.

Over the years, this culture permeated the organization with each person at a senior position in the company practising and propagating the value system in their sphere of influence.

The result of creating a non-evaluative culture has been evident in the agency in the form of a secure and nurturing environment, with no internal politics or turf wars, and an entrepreneurial spirit and shared values reaching down to the junior most levels.

Almost everyone who has been at Ulka will have stories of challenging times, both at the business and personal levels, and yet, have found a supportive environment to navigate through these periods.

I recall my early days at Ulka when I took over an office in decline and almost the entire team had either left or were in the process of leaving the agency. The talk of the town was how Ulka would close down in the next few months.

It was not a very encouraging situation to walk into. I recall Anil's (my boss) words to me, 'Do the best you can. I believe that you will do a great job of turning the office around—better than I or anyone else can. So don't worry about anyone evaluating you every day.'

It took almost a year and a half of 15-hour workdays, and a whole lot of sweat and tears to get the Delhi office to a survival level. During this entire period I was never once asked what the billings were expected to be in the next month or the next quarter.

Yet another similar situation arose almost after the difficult initial years when the Delhi office had built its business and reputation. By 1995, it was peaking, having set up a great team and securing a slew of new businesses that would have been the envy of any agency in the city. We had brands like Frito-Lay, Tropicana, HP, Vanish (Reckitt Benckiser), Whirlpool, etc., and all these were acquired locally with no global alignment. However, with FCB being taken over by IPG, all these businesses had to be given up due to global alignments and conflicts, resulting in a loss of revenue for Ulka, especially the Delhi office.

It was a very difficult time and the process of rebuilding the business was not easy but for the support and reassurance from everyone. There was a strong belief that we would once again succeed like we had before, which we did over the next three years with additions of clients like Hero Honda (returning after a gap of over 15 years), HCL, ITC (John Players) and Godfrey Phillips India (GPI). All this happened in a supportive environment with no pressure from Anil or my colleagues on the management board.

The turnaround started with our getting the Hero Honda business, which required two years of regular follow-up. Atul Sobti was the marketing head at Hero Honda, and when I first met him, he was very clear that Hero was not looking to add to its roster of agencies. If anything, they were keen to consolidate their business with fewer agencies. I told Atul that Hero Honda was special for Ulka, considering that we had launched the first Hero Honda motorcycle with the famous 'Fill it. Shut it. Forget it.' campaign way back in 1983–84.[14] I was determined to be on the Hero roster, and was waiting

---

[14]Hero Honda (CD 100), YouTube, https://www.youtube.com/watch?v=FrvRE5b7H8U.

for the right opportunity. All I asked was whether I could drop by and meet him every once in a while, and send over regular updates on our insights into the two-wheeler market, with no strings attached. Atul was gracious enough to agree. It took two years to be invited to pitch for a new model that Hero was planning to introduce. Ulka won that pitch and became a roster agency for Hero Honda.

The previous chapters have outlined the major attributes that made up the Ulkaway—how we interacted with each other and with our clients, how we took decisions, how we responded to change and how we rewarded our teams. The challenge was to fit all these attributes into a cultural style and then study its pros and cons and see how we, as an organization, were similar or different from others. This quest led me to go through a lot of published work on organizational culture, and the next chapter is about organizational culture models and how the Ulkaway fits into the conceptual framework.

ELEVEN

THE ULKAWAY

'Organizational culture is the sum of values and rituals which serve as "glue" to integrate the members of the organization.'

—Richard Perrin

Right at the outset of this chapter I must say that it is a bit more conceptual and less anecdotal than the earlier chapters. I have used some models of cultural styles available in the literature to determine the Ulka culture style. At the end of this chapter, I have attempted to summarize the pros and cons of the Ulkaway and how we worked to mitigate its disadvantages.

Culture is the informal, largely unwritten norm governing how people in an organization interact with each other and respond to change and the external environment. There is no singular 'right' kind of culture; different organizations have different kinds of cultures, each with potential for success. As seen earlier, what is more important is the synchronization between strategy, culture and leadership within the organization. There is considerable literature that exists to encapsulate the amorphous concept of culture and its various attributes into a cultural style.

Having delved into the literature, I felt that the Competing Values Framework was the best way to depict an organization's cultural style because it offered very distinct advantages. Cameron and Quinn outline six advantages in their book *Diagnosing and Changing Organizational Culture*[15]:

1. Practicality: It captures key elements contributing to organizational success.
2. Timeliness: The processes do not take too much time.
3. Involvement: It engages people within the organization who influence its direction and values.
4. Qualitative and quantitative: It can capture both the finer nuances as well as a broader viewpoint of the organization.
5. Manageability: It can be conducted by people within the organization without external help.
6. Validity: It is backed up by literature on the subject.

COMPETING VALUES FRAMEWORK

The Competing Values Framework was developed based on studies on organizational effectiveness[16] and subsequent work on culture, leadership and organizational structures.[17]

The Competing Values Framework identifies culture types based on seemingly competing work styles. The two axes

---

[15] Cameron, Kim S., and Robert E. Quinn, *Diagnosing and Changing Organizational Culture: Based on the Competing Values Framework* (Third Edition), Jossey-Bass, San Francisco, CA, 2011.

[16] Quinn, Robert E., and John Rohrbaugh, 'A Competing Values Approach to Organizational Effectiveness', *Public Productivity Review*, Vol. 5, No. 2, 1981, 122–40, https://doi.org/10.2307/3380029.

[17] Cameron, Kim S., and Robert E. Quinn, *Diagnosing and Changing Organizational Culture: Based on the Competing Values Framework* (Third Edition), Jossey-Bass, San Francisco, CA, 2011.

represent a spectrum spanning two opposite orientations. At one end of the spectrum are the orientations of flexibility, discretion and dynamism, whereas at the other end is the orientation towards stability, order and control. The second axis spans a spectrum from an orientation towards an internal focus, integration and unity of processes at one end, to an orientation towards an external focus, exploiting opportunities, differentiation and rivalry regarding outsiders at the other end.

These two axes create four quadrants, each typifying a dominant culture type.[18] The four quadrants are:

Dynamism/Flexibility

Culture type **CLAN**	Culture type **ADHOCRACY**
Orientation **COLLABORATE**	Orientation **CREATE**

Internal focus / Integration ←→ **External focus** / Differentiation

Culture type **HIERARCHY**	Culture type **MARKET**
Orientation **CONTROL**	Orientation **COMPETE**

Stability/Control

CLAN: THE ORIENTATION IS TO COLLABORATE

These organizations are like large families, where hierarchical relationships are characterized by benevolence, built on

---

[18]Cameron, Kim S., and Robert E. Quinn, *Diagnosing and Changing Organizational Culture: Based on the Competing Values Framework* (Third Edition), Jossey-Bass, San Francisco, CA, 2011.

a foundation of respect and loyalty. The expected mode is teamwork and collaboration. The environment is nurturing, fostering individuals to learn and grow for bigger responsibilities over time. Consensus-building results in common goals being achieved without excessive internal competition. While autonomy exists at business head levels, everyone is expected to strive collaboratively towards the larger organizational goal—capturing a spirit of 'one for all, all for one'.

These organizations adopt a long-term view, allowing them to withstand economic and market uncertainties due to the stability, commitment and loyalty of their employees. Promotions typically occur from within, with a focus on rewarding performance over time and demonstrating loyalty.

ADHOCRACY: THE ORIENTATION IS TO CREATE

These organizations mostly function in emerging technology areas or within the service delivery industry, operating in a fast-changing and competitive environment. They adopt informal structures with fewer hierarchies, fostering an environment where innovation, creativity and risk-taking are actively encouraged. Success in these organizations often result from breakthrough ideas and pioneering innovations in service delivery.

Entrepreneurship is the key driving force in these organizations, characterized by the ability to operate effectively in an uncertain environment where the risks are substantial, but the potential rewards of success are even greater.

MARKET: THE ORIENTATION IS TO COMPETE

These organizations are result-oriented and often operate in highly competitive environments, where monthly or quarterly target achievement is the key success factor. They consistently monitor changes in the external environment that can impact market share and margins. They keep a keen watch on competition and evolving consumer trends. The internal environment is demanding and performance is rewarded with better remuneration and promotions. There is a competitive spirit within such organizations, with team leaders motivating their teams to strive for victory.

HIERARCHY: THE ORIENTATION IS TO CONTROL

These organizations are process-driven, allowing very little room for creativity or flexibility. Once an efficient system is established, everyone is expected to operate within the defined parameters. Predictability is at a premium, and surprises or disruptive behaviour are not condoned. These organizations have well-defined monitoring and control mechanisms, with a focus on efficiency and stability. The objective is to ensure that an efficient and proven process is consistently followed for optimal results. A prime example of such organizations is the fast food industry, where the key successes are quality and efficient and timely delivery of service.

I have attempted to fit the Ulka values into the Competing Values Framework. To bring objectivity to determining the Ulkaway, I have supplemented my own understanding with insights from individuals who were at Ulka during the relevant two decades. Furthermore, I relied on the employee survey, which provides a wonderful insight into the culture as perceived by the Ulka team.

Considering that the employee survey, named Empover, was designed and implemented with the involvement of one of the most respected names in market research, Dorab Sopariwala, one can be assured of its objectivity and rigour.

The Empover survey was conducted biennially and I have taken the results from the 2009–11 survey.

The Research Design for Empover

- *A 51-point questionnaire*
- *Completely anonymous*
- *Nothing to be written (unless the respondent wanted to)*
- *10-point scale*

Confidence in Management

- *I trust in my management to always communicate honestly*   8.1
- *I trust and respect the top management of the company*   8.3
- *I believe the company values its people*   8.3

Learning & Nurturing

- *The agency is a great place to learn and grow in*   7.5
- *My seniors always give me the right direction and inspiration to produce great ideas*   7.2
- *My manager regularly coaches me on improving my performance*   7.0

Work Ethics

- *The company is clean, transparent and ethical in all its transactions*   8.5
- *People here are treated fairly regardless of caste, religion, gender*   8.7

Work Process & Infrastructure

- *The workplace allows me to be highly productive*   7.4

Openness & Change

- *The company encourages people to freely voice their opinions*   7.6
- *I feel encouraged to come up with better ways of doing things*   7.2

Teamwork

- *People in my work group work well together*   7.9

Growth & Career Path

- *I feel I have a bright future here*   7.4

Recognition & Reward

- *My seniors always appreciate my good ideas and give me credit for them*   7.7
- *The company always rewards good talent*   7.0

Clients

- *We handle some of India's leading brands*   7.8
- *I am proud to be associated with the brands I handle*   7.9

Engagement

- *I am proud to tell people I work here*   8.3
- *I feel a strong sense of commitment towards my organization*   8.1
- *I would recommend the company to others as a good place to work in*   7.8

ORGANIZATIONAL CULTURE ASSESSMENT INSTRUMENT

I also assessed the organizational culture at Ulka with the Organizational Culture Assessment Instrument (OCAI) proposed by Kim Cameron and Robert Quinn.[19] OCAI was developed to identify the cultural profile of an organization, and is one of the most used and useful frameworks in business (with over 10,000 organizations using it worldwide).

The instrument uses a series of questions across six cultural indicators.[20] Individuals are asked to rate their organization on these indicators: leadership style; the bonding mechanisms that hold the organization together; the strategic emphasis that defines what areas drive organizational strategy; the criteria for success that determines how victory is defined and what is rewarded and celebrated; the management of employees or the style that characterizes how employees are treated; and what the work environment is like. In combination, these indicators reflect the cultural values and reveal how the organization functions.[21]

---

[19]Cameron, Kim S., 'A Process for Changing Organizational Culture', *Handbook of Organizational Development*, Thomas G. Cummings (ed.), Sage Publishing, Thousand Oaks, CA, 2008, 429–45.

[20]Cameron, Kim S., 'Ethics, Virtuousness, and Constant Change', *The Ethical Challenge*, Noel M. Tichy and Andrew R. McGill (eds.), Jossey-Bass, San Francisco, CA, 2003, 85–94.

[21]Cameron, Kim S., and Robert E. Quinn, *Diagnosing and Changing Organizational Culture: Based on the Competing Values Framework* (Third Edition), Jossey-Bass, San Francisco, CA, 2011.

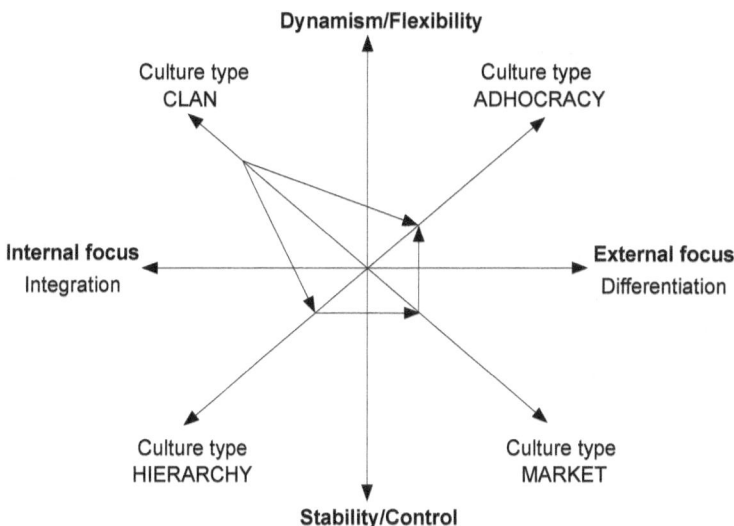

The above grid illustrates the Ulka culture profile as predominantly CLAN, with a strong emphasis on team excellence. In this culture, senior management played the role of mentors and coaches, fostering a high degree of commitment and loyalty. The senior team's long tenure in the organization, averaging over 15 years, highlighted the importance placed on attitude alongside aptitude and there were no overnight heroes or zeros.

While all cultural styles have positive and negative aspects, the critical issue is the synchronization between culture, leadership and strategy.

In contrast to typical advertising agency culture, which might lean towards the adhocracy quadrant in the Competing Values Framework model—emphasizing individuality, independence, flexibility and internal competition suited for the creative, award-winning campaigns that are the focus of these organizations—Ulka had a different focus. For us, the emphasis was on great strategy and providing holistic brand solutions, making a value mix of interdependence, collaborative teamwork and stability more effective.

Despite the emphasis on consensus building and a long-term view, which could have led to inertia in bringing about changes, Ulka overcame this potential obstacle due to its strong strategic focus. Anticipating changes in the advertising industry and planning for the future ahead of time became a key strength. For instance, Ulka pre-emptively separated media planning and buying from the mainline creative agency well before it became the norm, establishing LodeStar Media as an independent division. Similarly, Ulka was among the first agency groups to create specialized groups for direct marketing and event management—out-of-home and digital. The Group's second agency, Interface, designed to handle conflict issues, became a force in its own right with an enviable roster of clients. Thus, consensus building and advance planning were converted into a strength instead of a weakness.

The potential disadvantage of teamwork, rather than individual brilliance stifling creativity, was mitigated through transparency, fairness and equal opportunities for young talents. Ulka fostered a collaborative and open system for idea generation, where more than one creative team worked on major client briefs without turf or territory issues, allowing the best creative ideas to emerge.

The synchronization of leadership, culture and strategy hit a sweet spot, making Ulka unique and distinctive. This alignment resulted in over two decades of success. We will talk more about this success, exploring the effectiveness of campaigns and financial performance in subsequent chapters.

THE ULKA SUBCULTURES

The core culture at Ulka originated in the Mumbai office, where the senior team, excluding myself, was based. As a result, the attributes of the clan culture had the strongest manifestation in that office. However, the Delhi office, while closely linked to this core culture, developed a subculture of its own over a period of time.

This subculture came as a consequence of the unique nature of the Delhi advertising market. While Mumbai continued to be the dominant market for advertising, boasting established agency–client relationships, it was Delhi that saw the emergence of new-age categories such as computers, consumer electronics, telecom, online service start-ups and numerous multinational consumer product brands. Many of these new entrants sought fresh agency alignments and impactful creative strategies to achieve a high brand saliency in an increasingly competitive market.

While the Ulka positioning of providing brand solutions rather than just creative campaigns continued in the Delhi office, there was a need for a more aggressive approach to new business acquisition and enhanced creative impact to succeed in the Delhi market. This required the development of a subculture that encouraged creativity and greater responsiveness to market demands.

Hence, while retaining the core clan culture values of team spirit, loyalty, collaboration, interdependence and a focus on mentoring and nurturing, the Delhi office team developed its own sub-culture over the years. This transformation was the result of open discussions within the team on how to succeed in the competitive Delhi environment.

To shift the gear on creative output, the office brought in senior creative resources along with fresh young talent. An open, participative environment was encouraged, with elements of fun and frolic in the office, such as office parties, a pool table, birthday celebrations and open seating, contributing to a vibrant and informal atmosphere. I asked three creative directors to share their experiences of how it felt to work at the Delhi office. Reproduced below are their perspectives:

1. Shiveshwar Raj Singh (Shivi), the national creative head of Innocean and one of the creative directors at Ulka, Delhi, recounts one such instance.

I think it was 2007–08, when FCB Ulka, or Draftfcb as we had then recently been christened, had to suddenly and unceremoniously exit our Chandiwala office. This was the result of a sealing drive across Delhi that targeted commercial places operating in areas not earmarked for the same.

So while the hunt for a new office space ensued, we moved to a temporary shelter in the Okhla Industrial Area. This office was not really designed for an ad agency, to put it politely; it was rather characterless and bland, having possibly been a BPO set-up earlier. Naturally, it drew a none-too-favourable comparison with our recently vacated office. There were a lot of glum faces that trooped into this place, and overall, the mood was a tad downbeat.

That's how the idea of 'Thank God it's Friday' (TGIF) came about. I think it was Sanjeev Bhargava who initially came up with the concept. He roped some of us in to formalize it, give it shape and carry it forward—essentially, to liven up the atmosphere and get some positive vibes going in our slightly dull and drab office. While the name was borrowed from the famous diner chain, the content that we went on to create with our TGIF was totally original.

Roughly, this is how it all worked: every Friday, someone

had to get up and take centre stage somewhere physically in the middle of the entire office and stage a performance. It could be anything from a short skit to a play. You were free to recite a poem, sing a song or play the guitar. It could be anything, even a PowerPoint was accepted. The only guardrails were that it had to be relevant, fun and engaging for the rest of the agency folk. TGIF was to be our very own Hyde Park with free speech and fun demonstrations that were looked forward to by the entire office. Quite a few performances were witnessed. I think Sanjeev himself got the ball rolling and then nominated me for the next Friday's performance. Whoever performed would nominate the next week's candidate. The person whose turn it was could use the help of others to stage whatever they had in mind. Consequently, we saw some really cool takes on agency life. Digs were taken at clients and crazy deadlines. A lot of mimicry artists and hidden poets were suddenly discovered within the agency. We saw everyone from servicing, creative, planning and even finance under the ever-gung-ho Ravi Mehra get up and come up with some rib-tickling pieces.

TGIF lifted the spirits of the office tremendously. It became a fixture that really set the mood for the weekend. It made our Fridays memorable and Mondays a little less blue.

2. Vasudha Mishra, currently regional creative officer at Lowe Lintas, reflects on her years at Ulka Delhi.

I joined Ulka as a junior writer and left as the Delhi head. Thirteen years in one place—it was not an easy ride and had its fair share of bumps. But the people and the culture of the place made it happen.

Ulka, as I remember, was open, inclusive and not hierarchy-conscious. It had that comforting feeling, a place you could call home, where you could speak freely and maybe that's why think freely. It is largely because of this that we did the kind of creative work that pushed boundaries—Naukri.com, Jeevansathi.com, Tata Docomo.

Ulka Delhi also had an open-door policy. One could walk into Sanjeev's or Arvind's office any time—to grumble, catch up or just jam on ideas. I have ticked all three boxes.

I remember one incident: a junior writer (not me) had gone for a presentation and Arvind offered him a ride back in his fancy car. During the ride, the writer's date rang up. The writer spoke in hushed tones, apologizing for running late and assured his date that he'd soon be there. Arvind didn't ask any questions, being the gentleman he is. But as they reached the office, Arvind got off and instructed his driver to take the writer wherever he had to reach. So a junior writer went for his date in a fancy car.

A tiny incident, but perhaps indicative of a place that, for most of us who were there, no matter where our paths took us, we still think of as home.

3. Mehernosh Shapoorjee, co-founder of Mediation Mantras, member of the MediateIndia Advisory Board and at one time creative director at Ulka, shares his view on what made the Ulkaway distinct.

Corporate culture can make you compliant and follow established norms, or it can liberate you to be your best. Ulka was a very large joint family led by the patriarch, the late Anil Kapoor, based in Bombay. And Ulka Delhi was the extended quasi-independent nuclear family set up by Arvind Wable in another city. This led to the creation of a Ulka subculture in Delhi that was not far removed but clearly distinct from the culture in Ulka Bombay.

The three things that defined the work culture for me in Ulka Delhi are as follows:

New People, New Thinking

Not being able to draw from the heritage and reputation it enjoyed in Bombay, Ulka Delhi had to find and hire individuals who were unfamiliar with Ulka but were happy to embrace it for varying reasons. From a creative director's perspective, what I found invaluable was that Arvind Wable never insisted on hiring the 'Ulka type' of people. He only wanted them not to be divergently the opposite.

Young Blood, More Energy

The other interesting point about the culture at Ulka Delhi, particularly in the creative department, was the role and contribution of junior team members. Ulka Delhi hired and empowered a lot of youngsters who showed potential and allowed them to have a shot at big campaigns under the supervision of open-minded and secure leadership, which brings me to the last highlight of Ulka Delhi's culture.

Confident Leadership, Better Teamwork

We always had leaders who didn't suffer from personal insecurities and that really empowered people down the line to put in their best, knowing they would get credit where it was due. People like Arvind Wable and Sanjeev Bhargava were always open to people who challenged their thinking and shared ideas and opinions fearlessly. For instance, Sanjeev Bhargava wrote many of the lyrics for the Whirlpool jingles, and Mehernosh Shapoorjee provided strategic inputs and wrote creative briefs on many occasions.

We may have left the company for other jobs, but we're still at home with each other, with Ulka in our hearts and minds.

The outcomes were evident as the Delhi office successfully generated breakthrough campaigns. The initial projects for LML, Compaq Laptops and Tropicana signalled a significant change. Subsequently, outstanding work on brands such as Naukri.com, Whirlpool, Tata Docomo, HCL and Hero Honda set new standards for creative output over the next decade

What is even more impressive is that all these campaigns also won Effies, an award recognizing advertising effectiveness, thereby reinforcing Ulka's identity as a provider of brand solutions rather than just creative campaigns. Notably, the Naukri.com campaign[22] won an Asia Effy in Singapore. The Tata Docomo campaign[23] earned the India Grand Effie in 2010, and the client, Tata Teleservices, was declared the Effie Client of the Year. Thus, while elevating the creative quotient, the firm maintained a strong strategic foundation.

Culturally, the Delhi office created a subculture with a shift towards the adhocracy quadrant while retaining most of the clan values in the Competing Values Framework model.

---

[22] Naukri.com Hari Sadu, YouTube, https://www.youtube.com/watch?v=q6uYXDT9PyA.
[23] Tata Docomo—Friendship Train, YouTube, https://www.youtube.com/watch?v=a_v-SBZNMmw.

TWELVE

STRATEGY VS CREATIVITY

'Creative without strategy is called "art". Creative with strategy is called "advertising".'

—Jef I. Richards

Choosing between strategy and creativity is like choosing between mind and heart. Historically, strategy has long been seen as something that hinders, restricts or even kills creativity. So when an ad agency positions itself as being strong on strategy, the assumption often follows that it is not creative. What is surprising is how any right-minded creative individual can embark on a campaign without a clear strategy brief, outlining the key proposition.

In my opinion, asking creatives to work without a clear insight and brief is criminal. It is like shooting blindfolded in the hope that one will hit the target. In my experience, highly skilled creatives crave a clear, relevant and distinctive insight before diving into working on a piece of advertising.

This clear, relevant and distinct insight stems from a deep dive into the product category, the client, the competition and, above all, the consumer, which is precisely how we evolve a strategy—the backbone of advertising—a differentiated offering that sets a brand apart from its competitors.

Strategy defines what we want to tell the consumer, while a creative determines the how. If either one of the two is missing, we end up with work that lacks either a mind or a heart. Being mindless or heartless is certainly a considerable handicap for any brand. When strategy and creativity work in unison, we have a great campaign; otherwise, we might have mindless entertainment or heartless (skeleton-like) messaging.

Most seminal advertising campaigns often possess a magic that results from this seamless integration of strategy and creativity. The best creative directors have always understood the strategy behind the brand, often with depth and clarity surpassing that of many account planners.

Strategy serves as the foundation upon which the creative mind can soar—however, with a goal and a destination, rather than meandering aimlessly in pursuit of being different. Campaigns for Cadbury Milk Chocolate, Happydent, 'Hari Sadu' for Naukri.com, or 'When life can change in seconds, why pay in minutes'[24] for Tata Docomo—all had clear strategies and brilliant creatives, winning acclaim and awards for effectiveness and creative brilliance.

Creativity is not just about being different or whacky; it's about achieving a predefined goal in a refreshing, memorable, sustainable and uniquely different way. In advertising, creativity should not be a one-off, clutter-busting endeavour or solely about winning awards; it should be about sustaining a combination of good strategy and good creative over time.

At Ulka, strategy was the third pillar of success, complementing the other two pillars of leadership and culture. The strategic approach at Ulka was not centred on campaigns

---

[24]Tata Docomo: Pay Per Second—Aircraft, YouTube, https://www.youtube.com/watch?v=x4sL_bc64WQ.

but rather rooted in addressing marketing issues, consistently yielding measurable results. We need to consider a few examples to illustrate Ulka's focus on strategy and providing brand solutions beyond mere campaigns.

In the case of USHA sewing machines, the agency innovatively developed a range of coloured sewing machines to rejuvenate interest and infuse a fresh perspective into the brand. For the launch of Tropicana orange juice in India, Ulka recommended that the client limit mass media advertising and instead conduct a large-scale sampling exercise targeting a well-defined audience in metropolitan cities. Another illustration comes from the launch of the Hero Honda scooters, where Ulka recommended a bold approach to sharply segment the market.

These case stories span a period of 15 years between 1989–90 and 2006, showcasing the consistency of Ulka's approach to brand building.

PLEASURE SCOOTER: A CASE STORY

Why should boys have all the fun?

Hero Honda, the largest and most dominant player in motorcycles, strategically decided to enter the growing scooter market in 2005. Historically, the scooter category commanded a significant market share in the 1970s and 1980s, almost 80 per cent of the two-wheeler market in India. However, by the turn of the century, its share had dwindled to less than 20 per cent. This decline was attributed to a lack of product innovation in scooters and, significantly, the entry of fuel-efficient 4-stroke motorcycles in the early 1980s, spearheaded by Hero Honda itself, which launched its first motorcycle in 1983 with the iconic 'Fill it. Shut it. Forget it.' campaign created by Ulka. Hero Honda then went on to become the No. 1 brand and the largest manufacturer of motorcycles by volume sales globally, with over 50 per cent share of two-wheeler sales in India. Ironically, Bajaj, which had held approximately 80 per cent of the scooter market in the late 1980s, also lost interest in the category and followed Hero Honda into motorcycles.

The revival of the scooter category came with the introduction of lightweight plastic body 70cc–80cc scooters like TVS Scooty and the entry of Honda in the early 1990s with the larger, heavier metal-bodied 150cc scooters. While TVS Scooty and similar brands in the less than 100cc segment were positioned as unisex vehicles, Honda Activa was directed at the males and family segment.

Hero Honda wanted a significant share in the less than 100cc scooters, but was faced with the challenge of an undifferentiated product compared to the segment leader, TVS Scooty. The agency's task was to devise a strategic positioning and a creative campaign to meet this objective. In line with Ulka's campaign planning process, the agency team undertook an extensive customer study, utilizing proprietary tools such as VIP (visual profiling) and Mind&Mood, in addition to data provided by the client. Two crucial insights emerged.

First, the study revealed a connection to the economic boom in the post-liberalization era, fuelled by the technology and service sectors which, in turn, created job opportunities for suitably trained young individuals beyond the metros, particularly in Tier 1 and Tier 2 towns. For the first time, a significant number of young women were entering the workforce, requiring mobility and access to colleges, professional training and workplaces. However, due to the absence of a good public transport infrastructure in the country, there was a growing demand for personal transport in upcountry markets.

The second insight stemmed from the intensive work conducted by the agency's strategy team to understand the aspirations, motivations and constraints of young women in the context of the opportunities presented by the economic boom. One particularly striking revelation was the level of anxiety felt by young women about the differential treatment they experienced from their families, especially when it came to going out of their homes. There was constant monitoring of their whereabouts, their companions, the timing of outings and the mode of transportation. There was a strong insistence that they be dropped off and picked up by their father or brother. Notably, even younger brothers enjoyed more freedom of movement than the elder sister. Almost universally, girls had one question on their minds—why can't we do what boys in general and our brothers in particular are doing?

In its pitch presentation, the agency not only recommended the positioning for the new scooter but also outlined potential consumer segments and their sizes from which Pleasure could gain volumes. We were confident that we had the right strategy in place and that the creative campaigns would deliver the desired results. The campaign was not an end in itself; it had to deliver tangible and measurable outcomes.

Another interesting aspect was that the creative campaign for Pleasure, like many others, was a collaborative team effort in line with the Ulkaway. It involved two offices, one contributing the idea of 'Why should boys have all the fun?' and the other developing its rendition in the TV commercial featuring Priyanka Chopra.[25] More details on this collaborative process are presented in the next chapter.

The agency's sharply segmented approach, targeting young

---

[25]Hero Honda Pleasure (2006), YouTube, https://www.youtube.com/watch?v=HI5MmRYqfWA.

women instead of the diffused unisex positioning adopted by competitors, led to the liberating creative idea of 'Why should boys have all the fun?' The supportive market potential data, diligently analysed by the agency, convinced the client that it was worth taking the risk of a sharply segmented positioning.

The results were indeed spectacular: Hero Honda Pleasure surpassed its sales target, reaching 92,977 units in 2006–07, and emerged as the fastest growing scooter brand.[26] Furthermore, the same creative positioning was successfully refreshed in the subsequent three campaigns, propelling Pleasure to became the third-largest brand in the Hero Honda portfolio.

---

[26]Data provided by the Society of Indian Automobile Manufacturers.

USHA SEWING MACHINES: A CASE STORY

Going beyond just advertising

The sewing machine market in India was primarily dominated by a large unorganized sector, with small regional brands selling across the country, including the rural markets. The only two organized sectors that had established a strong brand presence were SINGER (Merritt) and USHA.

SINGER had been the pioneer, having invented the sewing machine and, at one time, held the dominant share of the organized sector brands in India. Over the years, USHA, with its extensive and efficient sales and distribution network, had become the leading brand. However, there had been almost no innovation in the category for over a decade and the traditional black, round-arm variety of machines continued to dominate the market. The advent of newer durables and changing consumer tastes towards ready-made garments had resulted in stagnation or, at best, sluggish growth in the sewing machine industry.

Around 1987–88, SINGER launched a range of automatic zigzag machines, refurbished the brand and started gaining market share from USHA, posing a threat to its leadership position. While USHA did have a semi-zigzag machine (Flora), it lacked an automatic zigzag machine in its range of products.

Traditionally, USHA's sewing machine advertising used a celebrity model to display garments stitched on its sewing machines. However, it became evident through extensive consumer contacts and internal discussions within the agency that a similar approach would not work in the face of the competitive challenge from SINGER. It became clear that USHA had to bring about some innovation in its product range. During discussions with the client and their technical teams, it was revealed that with over a hundred moving parts designed and perfected over 50 years, there was very limited room for product innovation in USHA's sewing machines. The breakthrough finally came from an unexpected source—the changes happening in other categories that had not innovated for a long time. A prime example was the age-old telephone, which had traditionally been black with a rotary dialling mechanism but had recently evolved into colourful phones with push-button dialling.

The agency came up with the idea of introducing a range of coloured sewing machines to infuse excitement and freshness into the USHA product line. The team at the agency actively sought out facilities that could assist in manufacturing these coloured machines, approaching specialized paint shops and decal makers. Within next four weeks, they successfully created a whole new range of machines in shades of red, blue, green and ivory, among others.

As per tradition, USHA used to conduct its annual advertising review in the Nilgiri room at the Oberoi Hotel in Delhi. The agency's office head (this time yours truly) made the presentation to the chairman of USHA, Lala Charat Ram, and the senior executive director, in the presence of the entire sales and marketing team. It was a grand affair, involving the agency team on one side and the marketing and sales team on the other, with the chairman, MD and other functional directors at the head of the table.

The presentation lasted 3–4 hours and included a detailed sales and marketing analysis of the previous years, leading up to the proposed marketing strategy and advertising campaign for the coming year. All the work presented had to be in its final finished form, including the final product shots intended for use in the campaign. Additionally, the agency had to create a full mock-up of a retail store adorned with all the proposed merchandise.

As the advertising strategy for the next year was presented, introducing the range of coloured machines, there was a moment of pin-drop silence from the client's side, especially the marketing team. The reaction from the MD and chairman was uncertain. As per the norm, the last part of the presentation involved a walk-through by the chairman and senior team of the retail store mock-up.

It was an extremely tense moment as Lalaji walked into the mock-up shop set up by the agency and saw the range of beautiful coloured machines on display. They could not believe their eyes. Lalaji was so impressed by the new range of machines that he promptly ordered his technical director to produce them on an urgent basis and launch them with a multimedia campaign.

The new coloured machines, named the GEM Collection, were successfully launched with a magazine and TV commercial campaign, resulting in providing much-needed freshness to the USHA sewing machine range. This initiative not only revitalized the relationship with the client but also led to the agency being awarded the significant business of USHA fans.

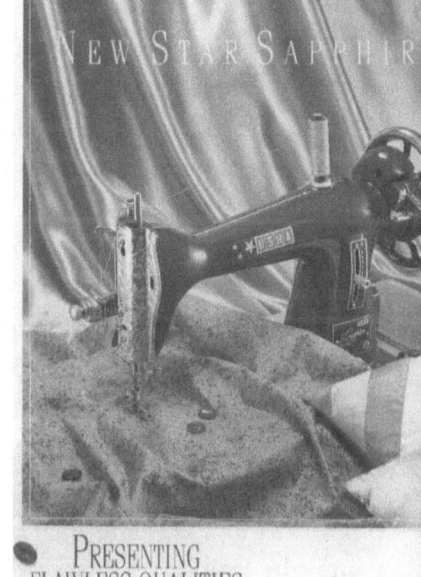

THIRTEEN

CREATING BRAND SOLUTIONS

'Making brands famous, making clients rich.'

—FCB Ulka

Ever since 1998, when the new leadership team took charge of the agency, there was a clear vision— to be providers of brand solutions rather than mere campaign suppliers. The focus was on generating success stories that showcased the agency's contribution, leading to a positive shift in tangible marketing parameters.

Within the initial twelve months, Ulka achieved two such landmarks. The first involved the repositioning of Santoor soap for Wipro's consumer products division. The shift from an ingredients-focused narrative to a benefit platform ('Meri twacha se meri umra ka pata hi nahin chalta') resulted in an immediate increase in sales.

The other case was for ITC, a tobacco company venturing into the edible oil market. The refined edible oil market, previously dominated by brands like Saffola, targeted the 40–50-year-old male susceptible to high cholesterol levels. In other words, the positioning was of a 'Healthy oil for unhealthy people'. Quite contrary to the accepted category platform, Ulka positioned ITC's new brand Sundrop as the 'Healthy oil for healthy people'. This unconventional approach propelled Sundrop to become the leading packaged refined oil brand. The television commercial (TVC) for Sundrop remained unchanged for nearly nine years and the positioning has endured for over two decades.

For the Delhi office, the big breakthrough came with LML scooters. The agency repositioned the product as a motorcycle among scooters for the young adult, differentiating it from the dominant legendary market leader, Bajaj scooters, who marketed their scooters as the family man's means of transport. This strategic move resulted in an immediate increase in sales and market share for LML, previously a marginal player with a chequered history despite spending large amounts on advertising.

These three case studies laid the foundation for numerous success stories in the years ahead, involving brands like Whirlpool, Tata Motors, Tropicana and Naukri.com. In every case, the agency contributed in a strategic manner, which positively impacted the fortunes of the brands.

LML: A CASE STORY

Building your own mountain

It was mid-1990, and over the past year the new team at the Delhi office had been seeking a breakthrough into one of the major accounts in the city. Although we had been invited to a few pitches and secured a couple of wins, we were still waiting for that big opportunity capable of truly turning around our business in the city.

The opportunity presented itself when we heard that LML

scooters was looking for a new agency, but unfortunately, we were not on the invite list. Despite this setback, we managed to secure an appointment with the advertising manager, who explained that the Ulka name had been considered but was dropped due to market rumours about the office's performance and the departure of most of the old team.

We somehow convinced him to grant us the opportunity to at least be invited for the pitch, to which he reluctantly agreed. The next three weeks became a whirlwind of activity, with 15-hour workdays, including the development of our credentials presentation to display our capabilities. During the initial two weeks, we put tremendous effort into understanding the market's competitive scenario and engaged with consumers to reveal new insights.

In June 1990, we were invited to make a presentation to the managing director of LML and the entire marketing team at Hotel Hyatt, Delhi. The presentation lasted over three hours, and by the end of it, we sensed that we had made a significant impression on the LML team. We were the last agency to present and were told that the results would be communicated by six o'clock that evening.

I still recall the entire team returning to the office and anxiously waiting to receive a call from LML. The call finally came at 6.30 p.m., informing us that while we had done a great job in terms of our strategy and creative campaign, the decision had been made to retain the account with their current agency. The only ray of hope we were left with was the comment 'Do stay in touch, we may want to consider you for other group companies.'

In the subsequent weeks, the new LML campaign was launched with great fanfare and we realized that the positioning adopted by the selected agency differed from our initial recommendation. We were convinced about the approach we had taken and did not give up hope. For the next year, we continuously stayed in touch with the LML team, providing inputs on the industry, new consumer insights and reiterating our point of view in terms of strategic direction as originally recommended.

We were often referred to as the 'alternate voice' at LML. To appreciate the positioning direction recommended by Ulka, one needs to understand the market situation at the time. The two-wheeler market was predominantly scooter-dominated, with brands like Bajaj holding a considerable share of over 70 per cent. The Bajaj Chetak, their bestselling model, was an iconic brand rooted in the 1960 Vespa range of scooters from Piaggio, Italy, which had been the technology partner to Bajaj. Ironically, LML was the current technology partner of Piaggio and had a range of scooters based on the 1980's technology. Despite being a superior product, LML could not establish brand superiority in the Indian market due to the stature and the trust consumers had on Bajaj Chetak.

During our pitch for the LML business, the brief clearly outlined the features that made the LML product superior to Bajaj. The LML scooter boasted better balance, superior brakes, improved lights and increased acceleration and the client expected the agency to develop a positioning that encapsulated all these product advantages.

The incumbent agency, which had won the pitch, opted for safety as the overarching positioning—a logical choice considering that better balance, lights, brakes and acceleration result in a safer scooter. The client had conducted research on safety as a parameter and consumers confirmed that LML was indeed a safer scooter.

The incumbent agency crafted a memorable film on safety,

which was remembered and liked by consumers in the brand tracking research conducted by the client. The TVC also won an award at that year's advertising awards. Consequently, the client was a little confounded as to why Ulka continuously believed that safety was not the right direction for LML. The irony lay in the fact that while positioning, creative work and research suggested that the LML product should perform well, sales and market share figures told a different story. After over a year of investing money in that direction, the client finally invited Ulka (the alternative voice) to present our point of view.

The Ulka strategy was based on the following insights:

1. Bajaj had a production capacity of 1,00,000 scooters a month, while LML's production capacity was only 20,000 scooters a month.
2. Bajaj, as an iconic brand, enjoyed strong customer loyalty, stemming from a great degree of satisfaction derived from product performance proven over two decades.
3. While safety was an important parameter when considering the purchase of a scooter, it was not a significant discriminator for brand choice.
4. Despite LML being perceived as a safer scooter in the research, the consumer did not view Bajaj as an unsafe scooter.

Hence, investing in safety as a key differentiator with Bajaj was not cutting much ice in terms of brand switch.

Ulka's recommendation had been to leverage Bajaj's biggest strength and turn it into a weakness. The vast base of Bajaj consumers consisted of families who, over the years, had bought a Bajaj scooter only. In many cases, families had used Bajaj Chetak since three generations.

The reason we felt this was an opportunity stemmed from the evolving preferences of young consumers in the country, who increasingly wanted to do things differently from what their fathers and forefathers had done. In other words, they wanted to stand apart as a newer generation, making unique decisions about their lives and the products or brands they associated with. This period also marked a shift among the younger generation towards motorcycles as a more trendy and hip mode of transport.

In essence, Ulka's strategy was to position the LML product as the 'motorcycle among scooters'. The client was nervous about this recommendation, as it contradicted traditional wisdom and stated consumer preferences as indicated in the category research available. In fact, they were so convinced of having a superior product that they wanted us to create competitive and comparative advertising directed at Bajaj. It took a lot of effort to convince them otherwise. Our contention was that attacking the market leader, which had tremendous consumer loyalty and affection, would be counterproductive. Instead, LML should position itself as the choice of the new generation. Our view was encapsulated in the heading of our presentation, 'Build your own mountain' (don't attack Bajaj, the big mountain). Regarding the consumer research that showed a preference for Bajaj's strengths, our view was that when one brand dominates the market, any research would inherently have a bias in terms of preference for the dominant brand, given that most consumers seek to rationalize their choices.

The premise was that we were not attempting to take away the core of Bajaj's loyal customer base. Our goal was to skim the outer layer, those seeking an alternative to Bajaj. We believed that this segment was large enough and more than adequate to make use of LML's production capacity.

After much debate, discussion and a series of presentations, LML agreed with our recommendation and we launched a new campaign supported by TVC, print and outdoor. We were also helped by the coming in of Mr Ravi Kant as the new marketing director at LML, who saw merit in the agency's perspective and agreed to the suggested positioning.

The new campaign portrayed one of LML's existing products, the T5, as the choice of the young generation. The TVC was shot in a style reminiscent of an MTV music video, with the lyrics 'It's got the power, it's got the style', set to a fast-paced music track.[27] The print ad resembled a motorcycle ad, showcasing a black T5 model of LML, beautifully shot with the words 'Style · Power · Performance'. The response to the campaign was almost immediate, and within weeks, black T5s became LML's hottest-selling model. Over the next two years, LML's share of scooters doubled without any changes to the product.

This case study marked a turning point for Ulka Delhi, and we secured several new businesses by presenting this case to prospects.

---

[27] LML Vespa Scooter Style & Power, YouTube, https://www.youtube.com/watch?v=bwWKdXmHQ7Y.

WHIRLPOOL: A CASE STORY

Uncompromising care

Between 1991 and 1995, LML was the major client of the Ulka Delhi office. The work undertaken for LML proved to be a game changer in the scooter category, earning the agency accolades in the industry and attracting new business based on the LML case.

However, it was time to pursue another major advertiser in the Indian home appliance market—Whirlpool. Whirlpool had entered India a few years earlier by acquiring the manufacturing facility of two companies: the Kelvinator plant in Faridabad and the TVS washing machine plant in Hyderabad.

The incumbent agency was strongly entrenched in the brand and required our relentless efforts for almost six months to secure an opportunity to present our credentials to Whirlpool.

Our approach in the credentials presentation was to emphasize the strong and committed team at Ulka and showcase the brand-building work we had undertaken for a whole host of brands, including LML.

The Whirlpool marketing head was open to considering Ulka's point of view but was reluctant to disrupt their existing agency relationship. It was agreed that Ulka would work independently without a specific brief from Whirlpool and also ensure that news of this assignment would not be leaked. Only three individuals at the Delhi office were aware of this assignment and all work would be conducted from our Bombay office. We also gave the assignment a code name—'Tolkien' (inspired by my reading of the book *The Lord of the Rings* those days). We were hoping to secure the business without an open pitch, but internal procedures at Whirlpool required them to invite pitches from at least three agencies before appointing a new agency partner. Two months later, a formal pitch request for proposal (RFP) was sent out by Whirlpool, inviting the top three agencies in the country, along with the incumbent agency, to be a part of the pitch. This obviously changed the odds for us.

Once again, instead of focusing solely on a fresh creative approach, we focused on getting the strategy and positioning right for Whirlpool. A detailed analysis of the current household appliances market, consumer behaviour, competition and the Whirlpool product portfolio was undertaken by the agency. We conducted a special study to understand the brand perception among target consumers using a differentiation ratio technique to arrive at the factors on which consumers differentiated brands.

A competitive brand analysis led to a positioning map and the potential gaps that Whirlpool could occupy. Interestingly, while factors like innovator, trust and style emerged as the strongest, we felt that Whirlpool could not claim any of these, as there were already strong competitors occupying these platforms (Sony—innovator, Godrej—trust, BPL—style). Despite being an established brand globally, Whirlpool was relatively unknown and new to India. Even at the global level, it was a trusted brand, but not necessarily an innovator or a stylish brand; instead, it was seen as a good quality, solid, mid-western American brand.

The breakthrough in positioning came from our understanding of the Indian consumer. Traditionally, household appliance brands had targeted the male consumer on the understanding that they had the deciding role in the choice of home appliance brands. However, our consumer studies revealed that housewives played an increasingly important role, not just in initiating the need for an appliance but also in deciding the model and brand to be purchased. Thus, we decided to shift our focus to the housewife rather than the husband.

The affinity and focus group studies undertaken by the agency provided some very interesting insights about women and their roles as housewives:

1. Many urban housewives had the education and qualifications to be working women but chose to take care of their families.
2. Even working women were expected to almost single-handedly manage household responsibilities in addition to their jobs.
3. All housewives felt that the housework they did was taken for granted by their husbands and children.
4. While they were content in their roles, they looked forward to being appreciated by their families.

In essence, the care provider was seeking care for herself. We felt that this strong emotional connection was a territory that Whirlpool could occupy by becoming the care provider to the housewife. The other key recommendation was to start referring to the housewife as a 'homemaker', someone who was the pivot and anchor on which happy families were built.

Hence, the three pillars of Whirlpool's positioning were:

1. A superior product based on Whirlpool's credentials as the world leader in home appliances.
2. Introducing the concept of 'homemaker' as the anchor on which happy homes are built.
3. Whirlpool being the partner of the homemaker.

From the above emerged the final positioning for Whirlpool in India, 'You and Whirlpool—the world's best homemakers'.[28]

---

[28]Whirlpool India—Brand Movie, YouTube, https://www.youtube.com/watch?v=1Bhksh_dnpA.

The other significant recommendation made by Ulka was that Whirlpool's media budget should focus on television rather than print. This was quite contrary to the practice for home appliance companies at that point in time, which used to spend almost 70 per cent of their advertising budgets on the print medium, essentially focusing on the features of their product. Our media strategy was aligned with our positioning and the need to create an emotional bond with the homemaker.

The final pitch presentation was an elaborate affair with the entire leadership team of Whirlpool present. Unlike other consumer durable or home appliance companies, the Whirlpool leadership team comprised seasoned professionals from multinational FMCG companies—HLL, Pepsi, GSK, Nestle, Colgate, etc. These individuals were well versed in brand marketing and posed tough questions. Our presentation, originally scheduled for 90 minutes, took almost three hours, during which we were questioned about our unconventional strategic approach. The fact that we stuck to our point of view showed the rigour of our analysis.

Whirlpool reverted to us within a week, informing us that we were the front runners in the pitch but there were some clarifications the team needed on our recommendations. One key requirement from the managing director was to provide in one line the core value of the Whirlpool positioning. We sent in various options but none were found acceptable. On the final day, while travelling to the Whirlpool office with our latest versions of the core values, two words struck me almost like an epiphany—'Uncompromising Care'. Whirlpool's care is like a mother's care—warm, affectionate and understanding but not at the cost of quality (uncompromising). Whirlpool home appliances give the homemaker a superior wash, cooling and cooking, not just convenience. Those two words clinched the Whirlpool account for us.

Another unique aspect of all Whirlpool advertising was that we used only one model for the role of the Whirlpool homemaker in all our advertising, creating a face identified as the 'Whirlpool mom'. The Whirlpool Homemaker campaign was a huge success. It introduced the term homemaker (instead of housewife) to the Indian advertising lexicon and created a strong emotional connect with the brand.

The work done for Whirlpool won the agency the first award at the Bombay Ad Club's 'Advertising that Works' Award show (the award later became the India Effie). The Whirlpool mom became one of the most recognized characters on Indian TV advertising, and the sign-off line 'Mummy ka magic chalega kya' became a popular catchphrase in the media. According to a survey by Milward Brown, Whirlpool became the most preferred brand for refrigerators and washing machines in 2003.

The Ulka–Whirlpool relationship lasted almost 20 years, creating a brand that withstood the might of the Korean onslaught (large advertising spending and continuous innovation) and continues to hold a significant position in the home appliance category.

These case stories depict the actualization of the Ulka approach to advertising and brand building with a focus on good strategic thinking and creatives that delivered results. Our recommendations were always based on a deep insight into the consumer and market environment in which the client was operating. The objective was not to create a great campaign but to help the brand achieve its marketing objectives. Hence, like our internal way of working, our relationships with the client team were collaborative; we worked as an extension of the marketing team, but with an independent perspective. One of the key values at Ulka was the integrity of advice, which required that we would never sell a campaign that we did not strongly believe would deliver results for the client. We would never sell a campaign because it would get us an award or more billing. This earned us the trust and respect of our clients, most of whom stayed with the agency for decades or more, and in many cases, including Whirlpool, preferred Ulka to their globally aligned agencies. Our strategy was clearly aligned with our culture of teamwork, cooperation and collaborative effort.

Kinjal Medh, who spent over two decades at Ulka, recounts this in his story of Anil Kapoor's vision and binding force of culture. Kinjal was the COO of Cogito Consulting at FCB Ulka, then chief marketing officer at the National Stock Exchange and is now a marketing consultant.

In my first meeting with Anil, he shared his own views, his vision and plans for the agency and why he was looking for people of a certain profile. He managed to convince me to give up a much better offer (from a then bigger agency) to join Ulka, an agency which I was repeatedly warned was on its last legs.

He had a vision and a plan, and it was only after a few years of working at Ulka that I realized he made sure Ulka walked every syllable of the talk he had given me that day. Anil's vision for an agency was to be a true strategic partner to clients, growing with the client's business growth rather than living from campaign to campaign. Anil would have been the first to accept that he could not achieve his vision single-handedly. He needed a team of believers, a team with the credentials to match their clients and provide genuine value additions and strategic insights. It was no accident that the entire top leadership team came with not just advertising creds but with prior stints in sales and marketing as well. It was a team that could speak the clients' language and understand their challenges and pain points, empathize with them and give them confidence; a team that had the passion for creative solutions that went beyond a script or a layout.

This belief and commitment had to reach right across the organization. He encouraged his team to build partnerships down the line. This ideology of 'partnership with clients, partnership with employees and partnership with associates' was not hung on any wall but roamed the corridors every day. And over the years, the outcome of this ideology became gradually visible.

The strategy of building and nurturing a team of believers paid handsomely as FCB Ulka built one successful business after another. Rather than recruiting from outside for specialized functions, FCB Ulka trusted talents from within—talents who pursued client success with the same commitment and passion, be it for Lodestar Media, FCB Ulka Direct, FCB Ulka Digital or FCB Ulka Healthcare. A strong belief in strategy planning and consulting led to the formation of Cogito Consulting, an independent marketing brand and competitive strategy business that also did projects for a lot of non-clients of FCB Ulka, and in fact for some direct competitors as well.

FCB Interface is a great example of how a second agency can succeed, provided its foundational ideology and business are based on strong principles and not as a tactical response to managing business conflict. It was a matter of great pride for all of us when a little more than a decade after the tie-up, FCB Ulka was awarded the best-managed agency in the FCB Worldwide Network and Anil became the first Indian to be invited on the board of an international agency network.

Anil believed that agencies were selling themselves short and had become mere suppliers of creatives. He urged agencies to not see their roles narrowly defined by a creative campaign or a film but a broader, more imaginative role as a provider of solutions.

Anil was neither a preacher nor a theorist. He just spoke about what he believed in strongly and what he had actually practised and delivered. It was a working model, a proven model, with which he and his team had revived FCB Ulka to make it one of the most respected agencies in India.

In many ways, the Ulka model was contrarian thinking and there will be many sceptics. But Anil has more than demonstrated that his vision could succeed, that there is an alternative strategy for the advertising industry to adopt; to take on the role of becoming strategic partners to clients rather than assume a narrowly defined role as a 'creative agency'. Anil strongly believed that the strategy to aspire for a 'virtuous cycle' could be a win–win for all stakeholders.

This is Anil's lasting legacy—a very successful agency is just the by-product.

Mr Ravi Kant, former marketing director of LML and former vice chairman/managing director of Tata Motors says the following about his relationship with Ulka and Anil.

An accidental encounter with Anil (Kapoor) and his team in 1991 in New Delhi morphed into a lifelong relationship. Whether in official capacity or outside of it, I have been fortunate to have enjoyed extremely warm bonds with a number of talented 'Ulkaites'; though too numerous to name all, I must mention Arvind, Nitish, Sanjeev, Radhika, Nosh, Aakash, Shikha, Roy and Praveen from Delhi and Anil, Shashi, Ambi,

Nagesh, Richa and Subodh from Mumbai. Anil and I became the best of friends and relied on each other as sounding boards for miscellaneous topics on numerous occasions. Shashi and I are on the advisory board of a non-profit in rural Bihar.

So how did it happen? I believe there were two factors:

One, strong mutual trust, based on consistent integrity, transparency, equity and authenticity, which led to a strong collaborative spirit reinforced by leveraging each other's strengths. It didn't require making an effort, as it was embedded in the DNA of Ulka culture.

Two, the above led Ulka to not have a narrow vision, limited to offering only creatives, but to have a holistic approach to offering solutions to grow the client's business. This melded the two organizations (agency and client) to go for and achieve extraordinary results.

Doing it silently without hankering for 'recognition' became the hallmark of the association, which is continuing to be nurtured even today, way beyond its 'official lifespan'!

Thank you, Ulka (now with FCB prefix), for this once-in-a-lifetime experience. I wish it all the best under its current and future leadership.

FOURTEEN

THE CULTURAL PAYOFF

'Culture is the magic start-up ingredient.'

—Colin Angle

Having gone through the Ulka story on culture, you may ask the question: how is what happened at Ulka more than a decade ago relevant to an organization today? I believe the importance of a clearly articulated and functional culture is as, if not more, important today.

Culture is an outcome of leadership styles. It needs to be nurtured so as to get firmly rooted within the organization. Culture needs constant nourishment to be kept alive and relevant through day-to-day practices, rituals, symbols, structures and rewards. This is why culture is intrinsically linked to leadership. The other critical linkage of culture is strategy.

Business leaders are vital to the creation and communication of their workplace culture. However, the relationship between leadership and culture is not one-sided. While leaders are the principal architects of culture, an established culture influences what kind of leadership is possible.[29]

---

[29]Schein, Edgar H., *Organizational Culture and Leadership* (Fourth Edition), Jossey-Bass, San Francisco, CA, 2010, xi.

Most organizations lay a lot of emphasis on strategy, and rightly so, but what is often missed is the interrelationship between strategy and culture. Strategy is a plan evolved from a mix of consumer insights, competitive advantages and market environment to achieve certain designated goals. Culture is a mix of values, beliefs, mindsets and social norms. Despite culture and strategy being inextricably linked, most organizations do not pay adequate attention to the culture. In cases where organizational culture and strategy are aligned, the beneficial outcomes are significantly higher than in organizations where there is a misalignment.

The current business environment requires not just great ideas to be competitive but better execution of strategies; it requires creativity and innovation in every aspect of business across the spectrum from product design to the ultimate customer experience. 'Corporate culture is, above all, the most important factor in driving innovation,' said Rajesh Chandy, professor of marketing at the University of Minnesota's Carlson School of Management.[30]

There is an evolution taking place in the aspirations and expectations across generations, spanning Millennials to Gen Z to Gen Alpha, which has made monetary rewards a hygiene factor for employee attraction, retention and productivity. The differentiators have shifted to the workplace environment and organizational culture.

Even when the workplace offers benefits such as flexitime and work-from-home opportunities, employee engagement reflects well-being above and beyond anything else. Material benefits do not result in employee loyalty. Employees prefer

---

[30]Craig, William, '8 Ways Company Culture Drives Performance', *Forbes*, Forbes Media LLC, 3 August 2017, https://www.forbes.com/sites/williamcraig/2017/08/03/8-ways-company-culture-drives-performance/.

something else to perks and pay: mainly, workplace well-being. And where does this well-being stem from? Positive culture. Period.[31]

Employees want a secure and safe environment to work in, where they have clarity regarding what behaviour is expected of them, what is encouraged and what behaviour goes against the organization's culture. They desire transparency in the reward system and clarity regarding career growth opportunities that are available to them.

In an open, transparent and fair environment, a team of believers is created, putting in their best effort to achieve personal and organizational goals. Employees become the best brand ambassadors of the organization, as we saw at Ulka.

There are numerous advantages to having a vibrant culture that is aligned with the strategic focus of the organization.

Culture provides stability through better retention and lower attrition, leading to a higher learning quotient. The knowledge acquired by experienced people remains within the organization rather than being lost due to brain drain. At Ulka, the senior management team, comprising the management board, business heads and department heads/team leaders, had an average tenure of 15 years or more with the agency, providing a competitive advantage in terms of cumulative experience in the industries/product categories they worked on. In many cases, the agency's experience in a category far outweighed the marketing heads' experience at the client's end.

Culture also provided Ulka an advantage in terms of recruitment and assimilation of newer people who joined. A

---

[31]Seppälä, Emma, and Kim Cameron, 'Proof that Positive Work Cultures Are More Productive', *Harvard Business Review*, Harvard Business School Publishing, 1 December 2015, https://hbr.org/2015/12/proof-that-positive-work-cultures-are-more-productive.

high employee turnover is a situation best avoided due to the material cost of seeking out, bringing aboard and training a new employee. This is especially beneficial at the management trainee level. The Star One programme for trainees at Ulka was designed to inculcate in them the organization's culture, creating a cadre of people who believed in the value system and became productive in a very short period of time with minimal adjustment issues. Hence, the high expenses involved in constantly looking for, identifying and training new employees were considerably reduced.

Culture results in higher employee motivation and satisfaction, leading to a sense of belongingness, better team dynamics and improved performance. A robust culture becomes the foundation of day-to-day work and decision-making shared across the organization. At Ulka, regular employee satisfaction surveys clearly showed high scores on all of the above.

A clearly articulated culture accepted within the organization makes it far easier to create a performance evaluation and reward system, establishing common yardsticks for success. At Ulka, the Partnership Programme espoused the values of collaboration, teamwork, interdependence, growth from within, rewards beyond just money, etc., making it easily understood and a motivating instrument for the employees.

Culture, with the buy-in of leadership in an organization, acts as a force multiplier, aligning leadership actions in accordance with the value system they propagate. The preaching becomes the practice and reinforces the culture down the line in the organization. A well-accepted culture mitigates the effects of different leadership styles/personalities, as leaders are seen to provide consistent and collaborative guidance and decisions.

In a word, organizational culture is the 'root' of the development of a company, playing a fundamental role from the individual employee level to the strategic implementation level. Most importantly, a positive organizational culture helps a company to strive and survive during market upheavals, while a negative or damaging organizational culture can destroy a company from its foundation. 'What's more, the organizational cultures provide not only a shared view of "what is" but also of "why is". In this view, organizational culture is about "the story" in which people in the organization are embedded.'[32]

A very tangible effect of culture is its impact on performance. There are various studies to establish the interlinkage between culture and business success, showing a strong and positive correlation between the two. The Ulka story over two decades demonstrates the link between culture and financial success. In 1990, profits seemed like a distant dream, with constant cash flow crisis and struggles to meet media payments and salaries. This was compounded by delayed payments by clients, which was an unfortunate practice in the Indian context. But we laid some basic principles consistent with our values, such as paying salaries on time, not defaulting on our media payments and never delaying vendor payments if cleared by the client.

The Ulka success story in tangible terms is evident from the sustained growth and profitability over two decades between 1990 and 2010. The gross margin of around 35 per cent year on year between 1995 and 2010 was way beyond industry standards. What is even more creditable is that this was achieved by a team of professional managers, none of whom had any shareholding in the business.

---

[32]Watkins, Michael D., 'What Is Organizational Culture? And Why Should We Care?', *Harvard Business Review*, Harvard Business School Publishing, 15 May 2013, https://hbr.org/2013/05/what-is-organizational-culture.

Nagesh Alai, the CFO and then chairman of FCB Ulka and co-founder of an AI start-up, amplifies how, like all other facets of the agency, even the financial aspects were aligned with our culture of doing business.

A conviction about the universal applicability of the finance principles to manage business and the potential to make a difference enthused me to join Ulka, a collapsing star much contrary to its etymology, plagued as it was by a bleeding balance sheet. The laconic, albeit clear, brief to me was to build a strong balance sheet.

It is anachronistic to have a view that businesses have a limited purpose of profits and the interests of stakeholders. No doubt, without profits no business can survive, and without financial prudence, no business can sustain itself over time. However, the key difference between a successful agency and a not-so-successful agency is in the approach to finances and financial thinking.

Profits are both the means and ends of any organization's purpose. Seeing means and ends in silos will be inimical to the organization in the course of time. To build a strong balance sheet, it is critical to realize this and bring about an attitudinal shift in the approach to and management of business.

Let me elaborate on this concept in the context of all the stakeholders who comprise the ecosystem, with some examples:

1) Clients/Customers

Means: Adding value to the client's business, sustainable and growing revenues, knowing the learning curve of the client's brands and bringing transparency and integrity in dealings.
Ends: Attracting and retaining businesses, building the client's brands, timely payments, being evangelists of our value proposition and sustained margins.

2) Media/Vendors

Means: Being the agency of choice for the best rates and spots, entering into long-term contracts and timely payments.
Ends: Client-specific specialized properties and getting the best business terms.

3) Employees

Means: Attracting and retaining talent, providing competitive emoluments, building a culture, training and development of employees' skills and employees sharing the spoils or stake.
Ends: Identifying with the vision and mission of the agency, teamwork orientation and motivation, feeling of belonging, accountability for business and growth and apolitical working environment.

4) Shareholders

Means: Sustained dividends, reinvestments into business, expansion of business, thinking and doing 'no separation of stakeholders and shareholders interests'.
Ends: Building an institution, sustainability of business and a strong balance sheet.

The annunciation of the above principles and living them as a way of life, whereby every single stakeholder, even with inherent and apparent conflicts of interests, ensured that the other's interests were taken care of and accorded primacy to the commonality of purpose.

The core nuance and essence was that while profits are essential, it will not be at the cost of any of the stakeholders; everyone's interests were scrupulously taken care of as a priority. Margins and profits flowed and a strong balance sheet was built.

FIFTEEN

PASSING ON THE BATON

In 2010, the transition of the team that assumed leadership in 1988 began. Anil retired in September 2010 as MD of FCB Ulka Group India and regional president of Draftfcb Asia Pacific and Africa. He moved on to a non-executive position as chairman emeritus of Draftfcb Ulka. As per the plan agreed upon two decades ago, the entire leadership team would give up their operational roles and retire upon reaching the age of 58, moving on to advisory and non-executive positions to facilitate the transition to a new leadership team.

A new direction for the agency was on the horizon, driven by a shift in the advertising industry over the last decade, gaining momentum with greater digitization and the entry of large-format retail, both requiring specialized services beyond traditional media. With greater digitization, technology and data were integrated into the mix of strategy and creatives.

The transition at Ulka took place with the realization of this shifting macro environment. Over the four years from 2011 to 2015, the existing leadership phased itself out in a manner that provided stability and continuity with minimal disruption in client relationships. The leadership team collectively and unanimously identified Rohit Ohri as the next CEO, expecting him to bring the necessary change required to align the agency with the changing environment while, at the same time, maintaining the core values that formed the Ulkaway.

Rohit Ohri assumed the role of MD and chairman of the FCB Ulka Group in 2016. In one of his first interviews, he acknowledged that he was joining an agency with a solid foundation and deep-rooted culture. He compared FCB Ulka to a book that had already been written, with him writing a new chapter to take the story in a new direction.

Over the last eight years, the new chapter has unfolded, and today, the FCB Ulka Group is an interesting amalgamation of the old and the new. The agency has retained a strong strategic focus for its marquee clients like Tata Motors, Amul, the Mahindra Group and others at its flagship Mumbai operations. The senior leadership team at FCB Ulka and FCB Interface, almost all of whom have been with the agency for 15–20 years or more, have provided continuity with deep client relationships, and continue to be the engines of growth and revenue generation. The induction of new creative talent has raised the creative bar and given a fresh look to the work emanating from the FCB Ulka Group.

The Delhi operations of the agency were revamped to align the agency with its global vision of outstanding, award-winning creatives by bringing in fresh talent to spearhead the creative thrust for the FCB Group in India. FCB Ulka is considered a top creative agency group in India and in the global FCB network. It boasts a string of awards at every international award show.

Lodestar, the media arm of FCB Ulka, is part of Mediabrands India, led by Shashi Sinha as CEO. A separate entity in the IPG worldwide network, Lodestar is a great success story in the media world and one of the largest media agencies in India.

Looking at this from a cultural lens, it presents an interesting mix of clan and adhocracy cultures with a combination of collaboration and creative orientation. While the older flagship offices, FCB Ulka and Interface, continued with their respective leadership teams and culture, the agency built a completely new team in Delhi with a very different positioning. Though this change in Delhi did cause disruption in existing client relationships and ultimately some loss of business, the new team, with its focus on award-winning creatives, picked up new business over time.

This has been a structural solution, where instead of disrupting the current leadership, strategy or culture of a very successful model for over 25 years, a new entity under the same brand name was created with a new set of leadership, strategy and culture at a different location. In effect, there are now three different agencies: FCB Ulka and FCB Interface based in Mumbai from the old stock of Ulka, and FCB India based in Delhi, drawing inspiration from the global vision of FCB worldwide. This has provided a path for stability and growth for the agency over the last eight years and has added a creative sheen to the FCB brand in India.

This capacity to adapt to a changing environment by altering strategy, leadership and culture has resulted in Ulka likely being the only independent Indian agency brand of the 1960s that became a major mainline agency and has retained that position for over 60 years.

In conclusion, I would like to go back to where I started, which is the title of this book, and reiterate some of the salient aspects.

1. The title *Culture Eats Creativity for Lunch* was an effort to bring culture into focus as the most critical component of organizational success. It is not to take away from the importance of creativity or other key ingredients like leadership, strategy or innovation.
2. Culture is the binding force that holds all other ingredients together. It is the unwritten norm of how people in an organization interact with each other and respond to external factors or changes. In the absence of a strong and positive culture, it is unlikely that any organization will be able to achieve sustainable growth.
3. Culture is not a constant; it can and should change or adapt if there is a significant change in the organization's operating environment.
4. There is no one right culture style; it depends on the kind of environment the organization operates in—its strategy and leadership style.
5. Culture is the result of deliberate and consistent action and day-to-day behaviour, especially by the leadership of the organization.
6. When leadership, strategy and culture are in sync, we have a Goldilocks moment or a situation when everything is just right for success.

The Ulka story of over 60 years is just an illustration of how a strong and positive culture, committed leadership and a unique differentiated strategy have resulted in the organization's sustained growth. I hope that this book kindles interest in organizational culture in the Indian context because culture is as much, if not more than ever, relevant in today's rapidly changing environment.

APPENDIX

REMEMBERING BOSS

Boss, as we at Ulka referred to Anil, lived his life kingsize. He was a big man with an even bigger heart. His zest for life was contagious; every moment spent with him was a learning experience. There was no middle ground for Anil; he passionately dived into every aspect of life, be it work or play. He either loved you or tolerated you or refused to meet those he did not like. Anil was a great conversationalist; one could spend hours with him and never get bored. He had stories, anecdotes and experiences to share. What made it easy to be with him was that you did not have to say very much; just sit back and listen.

Any issue of significance for Ulka was discussed and debated at great length. For those of us who worked closely with him, these sessions were called paathshala. It would start after office hours and go on for endless hours, interspersed with cups of tea, biscuits or namkeens, and invariably end up with dinner in the office or across the road at the Oberoi or at the Khyber at Kala Ghoda, followed by a stop at his favourite paanwala at midnight or beyond.

No discussion was confined to the narrow issue at hand.

Every aspect related to the issue, be it global, national, political, historical or philosophical, was discussed thoroughly before any direction or decision was taken on that issue. And participation of the entire senior team was required, and for anyone not participating in the discussion, Anil had a favourite quip, 'Muh mein dahi jamake baithe ho kya?' (Are you setting yoghurt in your mouth?) These discussions spanned clients, campaigns, strategy, industry issues, reward policies, etc. But the common theme underlying all this was the Ulka values and culture.

While I have tried to capture the salient aspects of this culture in this book, the richness of it could only be felt in Anil's paathshalas. I have taken a very long time to complete this book, partially due to laziness but largely because I always felt that my words were not capturing all the experiences of living with the Ulkaway. The one thing that kept making me go back to writing was my promise to Anil to complete this endeavour. My regret is that Anil passed away before I could fulfil the promise. But I will not forget the last time I met him in Singapore, and among other things, he said to me, 'Why don't you finish the book? I have been through the manuscript. I think it's good to go…' I promised him that when we meet next, I will have the book done. Unfortunately, that was not to be.

But I know wherever Anil is now, he is enthralling his audience with a lively discussion, and I need to be ready for my paathshala on the Ulkaway.

In remembrance of Anil, I am reproducing some of the tributes written for him on his passing on 12 April 2021.

Left to Right: Niteen Bhagwat, Ambi Parameswaran, Arvind Wable, Shashi Sinha, Anil Kapoor and Nagesh Alai

The definition of a friend is someone who is unafraid to give you honest advice. By that yardstick, Anil was not just a business partner but a true friend. From the first time I met him, he gave me fearless and candid inputs on our company and hence I counted him as a trusted adviser and friend. I will miss him greatly.

—Anand Mahindra
Chairman, Mahindra Group

Amul, one of Ulka's oldest clients, put up this hoarding in Mumbai as a tribute to Anil.

In the 1980s, what separated Anil Kapoor from the rest was the fact that all the established advertising agencies were headed by creative people, while Kapoor was from a sales and marketing background. He brought more MBAs and IIM passouts, basically people from the marketing background, in his team. I remember in all our advertising campaigns and meetings he used to say that creativity is a good thing for any campaign but it should ultimately serve the purpose of marketing to achieve the sales targets. It has to be centred towards sales creation, not only creative.

—**R.S. Sodhi**
Former Managing Director, GCMMF (Amul)

ZEE's journey with FCB Ulka has been long and fruitful, one that went beyond just a business association to a close-knit partnership. At the heart of this partnership was not just a thorough professional but also a very dear family friend, Anil or Billy as we fondly remember him, with his unabashed style and optimistic spirit. He was the one who fearlessly said what you needed to hear and not what you wanted to hear! In fact, he was amongst the few people who recognized my potential at the start of my career and encouraged me to take risks. The nuggets of wisdom shared by him over nuggets of scrumptious food on our plates were many! It is famously said that the way to a man's heart is through his stomach, and this was absolutely true in Anil's case! I think the fondest conversations with him were always over a delicious dish.

He was very passionate about three things—food, cricket and advertising. The culture that he instilled in FCB Ulka, an agency that was his child, was one that nurtured a deep understanding of clients, coupled with a passion for identifying intricate nuances. This resulted in the creation of some of the most memorable campaigns for us, including ZEE's 'Vasudhaiva Kutumbakam—The World Is One Family', which struck a chord with our viewers and partners across the globe. I vividly remember the moments leading up to the launch of this campaign and our edgy nerves. The talented and experienced team built by Anil ensured that this campaign and several others that followed were always executed in the best manner. Together as an industry, we can collectively agree that under Anil's staunch leadership, FCB Ulka has made a significant mark in the world of advertising. Today, as I remember Anil, I deeply miss the entertaining conversations on movies and cricket with a lavish spread that I will always cherish. Anil, you will always continue to live in our hearts for times to come.

—Punit Goenka
Managing Director and Chief Executive Officer,
ZEE Entertainment Enterprises Ltd.

FCB INDIA'S SUCCESS IS A TRUE TESTIMONY TO ANIL KAPOOR'S VISION AND GENIUS[*]

Sharing his memories, Rohit Ohri, then group chairman and CEO of FCB India, recalled a meeting he had with Anil Kapoor before taking charge of FCB Ulka in 2016.

'Mein tumhe apni beti de raha hoon.' (I am handing over my daughter to you.) This is what Anil Kapoor said to me when I took over as group chairman and CEO of FCB Ulka in 2016. Ulka was the daughter he had loved and nurtured for almost three decades.

He asked me to meet him for an afternoon coffee and our conversation took us almost to breakfast the following day! His passion for the agency and brands that he had built was evident. Listening to him as he ran me through the history of Ulka was a masterclass in the Anil Kapoor school of advertising. He was a fearless man who always believed in doing the right thing. His razor-sharp mind would first interrogate the business model and product delivery before thinking of communication, getting many a client to re-evaluate their marketing strategies.

Thank you, Anil. For sharing with me the 'secret sauce' that made Ulka what it is. And, for trusting me with your daughter.

—**Rohit Ohri**
FCB Global Partner

---

[*]First published by *e4m*.

ANIL KAPOOR—A SEEKER WHO THRIVED IN THE COMPANY OF IDEAS*

While I was trying to navigate and learn the ropes of the advertising industry in Mumbai, I was fortunate to have met Anil Kapoor. Unlike many ad people I met in Mumbai, whom one struggled to connect with, Anil reached out and made himself available to a relative newcomer.

I remember his call after my campaign for Coca-Cola (Thanda Matlab…). He had loved the work and organized a dinner, inviting the industry to celebrate the campaign. It was truly refreshing for me to see this level of large-heartedness. Anil was not in my company; he had nothing to do with Coca-Cola as a brand. Yet, overwhelmed by the creative work, he honoured and celebrated it. It was a gesture of a passionate and generous man.

Subsequently, we spent a lot of time together—with him and his family—an exceptionally connected family who took an interest in each other's work and valued it. Rita is one of the warmest hostesses and made my wife Aparna and me feel at home in a new city. His talented son Ram and daughter-in-law Gautami must have made him proud with their strides in the acting arena.

Deep down, Anil was a seeker and thrived in the company of ideas. His face would light up when I shared something fresh—a story, an anecdote, a poem. He would genuinely appreciate it. In fact, he'd follow up to ask if that idea or creative work had seen the light of day. He was not satisfied merely with lofty ideas and esoteric dinner party conversations; he believed in execution. This is the reason he left a vast legacy in the form of the agency he built.

---

*First published by *BW Marketing World* on 13 April 2021.

We also had another thing in common. We were equally passionate about the nuanced creative work India produces, which often goes underappreciated globally. Today, we have come a long way from that situation. In those days, Anil was one of the first people who represented India in Cannes as a jury member. He reminded me of this when I was chairing the Titanium jury years later. I remembered how passionately he would present the cultural context of Indian ads to other jury members. He really cared for the advertising profession and took pride in the work the industry did. Though over the last few years I could not spend time with him. Even on long-distance calls, I couldn't help but admire how determined and optimistic he was despite his health taking a downward turn.

People like Anil Kapoor are large—of heart and in spirit. And his legacy shall live on.

—**Prasoon Joshi**
Chairman APAC (Asia Pacific) and CEO,
McCann World Group India

A MAN WITH A GOLDEN HEART*

One of the things that anyone who's in a leadership role can take away from his (Kapoor's) life is how he inculcated the spirit of teamwork, held a team together and stood by his team. I could feel it without being a part of that organization. I could sense it from the way they bonded. The arguments must have been there. But that's what a team is all about.

He was also the first one to celebrate whenever someone achieved something. A man with a golden heart, a big heart. He took joy in the success of other people. When our agency won at Cannes, he celebrated the victory in his own house when we were not even a part of his agency.

—Piyush Pandey
Chief Creative Officer, Worldwide, Ogilvy

---

*First published by *ET BrandEquity*.

CONSENSUS, COLLABORATION AND CRICKET: REMEMBERING ANIL KAPOOR[*]

In 1988, when a marketing and sales guy was called in to revive Ulka by its legendary founder Bal Mundkur, the avant-garde, glamorous, laid-back world of Indian advertising didn't even bat an eyelid. The competition had already started writing Ulka's epitaph when Anil Kapoor made his luminous debut to save the day.

The Boots man entered the industry like a tornado and achieved the unimaginable with his aggressive, arduous, unapologetic and unique leadership style that was unseen and unheard of by the adlanders or their clients. Two of the pillars of his success were collaboration and consensus—the two basic tenets on which he rebuilt Ulka and its client relationships.

Anil had a well-rounded personality and tremendous knowledge about the advertising business. He always told us that we should know more about the client's business than the client himself. He built Ulka and the client relationships on that very philosophy. Very often, he would land in the client's office to discuss how they ran the business, to talk about their industry and the challenges. At first, many clients viewed this as pure arrogance. But when Anil started delivering the numbers, the same clients turned into his lifelong friends, and for some, Anil turned into a business adviser.

When we won Amul, one of the reasons Dr Verghese Kurien gave us the account was that we were not a multinational. So when Ulka got into the partnership with FCB, Dr Kurien called us, and we most certainly expected

---

[*]First published by *IMPACT* on 21 April 2021.

fireworks. At the meeting, Anil gave such a passionate speech that it even moved a strict leader like Dr Kurien, a man who always stood by his principles above anything else. He did not sack us but took away part of the business. Because of Anil's passionate argument, we got away, in Dr Kurien's words, 'with a rap on the knuckles'. In just one year, we won back several other businesses from Amul. Till today, 'The Taste of India' remains the primary tagline of the brand built under Anil. The relationship resonates in the unprecedented tribute that Amul put up for him with their iconic Butter Girl.

Like Kapil Dev once said, 'If you play good cricket, a lot of bad things get hidden.'

As for consensus, let me narrate a story. Usually, Anil would come to the office post noon and every evening, he would call 4–5 of us, his core team, and engage us in a debate. These meetings would last at least for 4–5 hours. If Anil saw that we were reaching an agreement in half an hour, he would fuel it further with a fresh debate so that it continued. If he was speaking and we sat quietly without participating, then he would yell. Every day we reached home around midnight, battered, but came back with equal enthusiasm the following day. And there were two reasons for that.

First, every decision we arrived at was of the best quality. Second, everyone had a sense of ownership in those decisions. There was not a single day when 'Boss' dictated and we simply executed. As a leader, Anil was way ahead of his time. He inculcated the spirit of entrepreneurship when such a thing in advertising didn't even exist. He would passionately speak about concepts like mindset management.

Today, each of the top 15–20 people Anil nurtured at Ulka holds a C-Suite position and they all follow in his footsteps in terms of running the business. Anil strongly believed that advertising, like cricket, is a team game. If you want fame for yourself, go play an individual game.

Anil also was a great believer in 'biradri' and it didn't mean just Ulka and its people. He was truly passionate about the advertising business and was extremely proud of our industry. So it could be Piyush or Prasoon winning awards. But the party was always at Anil's house.

He often told me that his two role models were Dr Vikram Sarabhai and Dr Verghese Kurien. While his food stories have travelled far and wide, very few know that he was a great sports enthusiast. He travelled all around the world to watch sporting events. Anil and I shared a great love for cricket and I had the good fortune of travelling with him to London, South Africa, Sri Lanka and many other places to watch the game. In 1999, we were in England for the World Cup when Anil's father passed away. Even though he would have been deeply disturbed, he didn't want to spoil my fun and planned to leave discreetly. It's another matter that I got to know.

He lived his life king-size and has left an unparalleled legacy. And as they say, a good cricketer never loses his nerve. Hope he continues his power-hitting in this new innings as well!

—Shashi Sinha
CEO, IPG Mediabrands India

A LIFE, LARGER THAN LIFE*

Anil Kapoor was a large-hearted person with strong values and a larger-than-life personality. There were no half measures in his vocabulary, whether it was the workplace or in his personal life.

His love for food and good conversation is legendary. Once we happened to be in New York and Anil invited my wife Neerja and me for lunch at his favourite South Indian restaurant. We got to the restaurant around noon; Anil was waiting for us with three glasses of mango lassi as a starter. As time went by, almost the entire menu was ordered and consumed largely by you can guess who! After some time, we saw that we were the only people in the restaurant and the staff were changing the table covers and laying out fresh candles. That is when we realized it was six in the evening and time for dinner. Conversation with Anil was always fun and easy as he did the talking and you listened. In the six hours, Neerja and I together probably got in six sentences.

At work, Anil's strong values were ingrained into every aspect of the culture at FCB Ulka. Integrity of advice and courage of conviction became the foundations of the turnaround and success of the agency.

One instance was when Sanjeev Bhargava was heading the Calcutta office and had after months of struggle landed a new client based on a brilliant campaign for a new product launch. Anil was visiting Calcutta so Sanjeev proudly took him to meet the client MD. When Anil heard the client's marketing plan, he told the client, 'Please don't waste your money advertising this product, it will never be a profitable

---

*First published by *IMPACT* on 21 April 2021.

venture.' A few days later, the company scrapped its plans to launch the new product. Sanjeev went back to chasing new business. Anil insisted that we should never do a campaign that benefits the agency in billing or awards but does not meet the client's marketing objectives.

Anil, for me, was much more than a boss, he was family. He was my mentor, guide and go-to person for every aspect of my life. During his last years, we got to spend time together, and I realized how wonderfully he had transited from his successful corporate life to an almost spiritual one. He often talked about vanaprastha or retiring to a distant land. I learnt an unimaginable amount from him both at a professional and personal level. I deeply miss his presence in my life.

—**Arvind Wable**

ACKNOWLEDGEMENTS

The Ulkaway has been a collective mission, which would not have been possible without the help of a lot of people. First and foremost is Anil Kapoor (Boss and Anil Bhai to me). Without him, the idea of Ulkaway would not have taken shape. I owe him the confidence to start this endeavour and his guidance throughout this journey.

Ambi (M.G. Parameswaran), with his extensive authorship of over a dozen books, has been my go-to person at every stage, from the first draft to structuring the book and advice on publishing. Ambi has also contributed his experiences of the Ulkaway and interesting anecdotes.

Niteen Bhagwat, Savita Mathai and Kinjal Medh helped bring together their perspectives on the Ulka values and shared their stories of their years at Ulka. Nagesh Alai provided a unique perspective on aligning finance and culture. C. Suresh dug out 20-year-old financial data for me to establish the link between performance and culture. Nitish Mukherjee shared his memory of our early days and how we worked together to build the team at the Delhi office. Sanjeev Bhargava shared his experience of trust and faith in the Ulka values. Mehernosh Shapoorjee, Vasudha Mishra and Shiveshwar Raj Singh contributed to the creative outlook and culture interface. Anirban Chatterjee and Mehernosh were among the first to give me feedback on the early chapters, with Ekta Verma formatting them into a dummy booklet to give tangible shape to my handwritten manuscript.

I want to thank my friend and batchmate Rajeev Batra for

reaching out to Professor Kim Cameron at the University of Michigan for some of his published papers on the Competing Values Framework and I am grateful to Professor Cameron for being kind enough to share them with me. I am honoured that he has written a foreword for this book. I could not have asked for a better endorsement.

My thanks to Mr R. Srinivasan (Ambi) who took an interest in *Culture Eats Creativity for Lunch* and directed me to Aditi Sriram at a stage when I felt bogged down with the writer's block. I needed someone to give me objective feedback, guidance and suggestions on the manuscript, its flow and structure. Aditi took time to read every line, every word of the manuscript and gave me very specific inputs. Thank you, Aditi, I could not have gotten unstuck without your help.

Rajiv Inamdar shared his experience and the pitfalls of self-publishing. Ashutosh Garg took time to go through the manuscript and was generous in sharing his contacts with publishers and recommending me to Dibakar Ghosh at Rupa Publications.

Shashi Sinha is the man you go to when all doors seem closed, and in his inimitable understated style, he opens up avenues that one does not know existed. Thank you, Shashi.

I express my gratitude to Rupa Publications, particularly Dibakar Ghosh, for his understanding, patience and guidance in bringing my mission to publish *Culture Eats Creativity for Lunch* to fruition. Special thanks to Shatarupa Dhar for meticulously editing the manuscript.

Finally, I want to thank my soulmate, friend and conscience keeper, my wife Neerja, for her encouragement, honest critique and patience on this decade-long journey. I am blessed to have children and grandchildren whose affection is a constant source of joy and cheer in our lives.

www.ingramcontent.com/pod-product-compliance
Lightning Source LLC
Chambersburg PA
CBHW030227170426
43194CB00007BA/884